BILLY SLATER

FROM NORTH QUEENSLAND TO
MELBOURNE STORM'S NUMBER ONE

BILLY SLATER

JOHN ELLICOTT

hardie grant books
MELBOURNE · LONDON

Published in 2014 by Hardie Grant Books

Hardie Grant Books (Australia)
Ground Floor, Building 1
658 Church Street
Richmond, Victoria 3121
www.hardiegrant.com.au

Hardie Grant Books (UK)
5th & 6th Floor
52–54 Southwark Street
London SE1 1RU
www.hardiegrant.co.uk

All rights reserved. No part of this publication may be reproduced, stored in a retrieval system or transmitted in any form by any means, electronic, mechanical, photocopying, recording or otherwise, without the prior written permission of the publishers and copyright holders.

The moral rights of the author have been asserted.

Copyright text © John Ellicott 2014

A Cataloguing-in-Publication entry is available from the catalogue of the National Library of Australia at www.nla.gov.au
Billy Slater
ISBN 9781742707457

Cover design by Bluecork Design
Typeset in 11.5/18 pt Sabon by Kirby Jones
Printed in Australia by Griffin Press
The paper this book is printed on is certified against the Forest Stewardship Council® Standards. Griffin Press holds FSC chain of custody certification SGS-COC-005088. FSC promotes environmentally responsible, socially beneficial and economically viable management of the world's forests.

CONTENTS

Foreword Beyond the Pain Barrier		7
1	Wild & Cheeky	11
2	Paellas, Potatoes & Footy	21
3	Billy on Track	38
4	Melbourne	68
5	Dazzler	95
6	A Rose for Billy	126
7	Annus Horribilis	150
8	Glory Days	170
9	Lapping it Up	189
10	You Know Who	213
11	Caught in a Storm	227
12	Resurrection	244
13	Tough as Teak	266
14	Riding on Horses	281

ACKNOWLEDGEMENTS

I would like to thank all the people who helped make this book possible and also acknowledge the journalists who gave of their wisdom and allowed me to use some of their material. They include Paul Kennedy, Brad Walter, Roy Masters, Mark Fuller, Stathi Paxinos, Brent Read, Debbie Spillane and Steve Mascord. Additionally, I would like to thank my publisher Pam Brewster and my family. I would also like to thank all things Sweet.

FOREWORD BY BRAD WALTER

BEYOND THE PAIN BARRIER

Of all the superlatives used to describe Billy Slater, 'toughness' wouldn't be at the top of many people's lists, but that is the first word that enters my mind when I think of the scrawny track work jockey from Innisfail who has become arguably the greatest fullback to ever play rugby league.

Having reported on Slater's career from the time he burst onto the scene as an 80 kg trialist for Melbourne Storm at the 2003 World Sevens series in Sydney, I have been privileged to witness many of the highs and the lows of a remarkable career in which he has been awarded a Golden Boot as the world's best player, Clive Churchill Medal for man of the match in a grand final and Dally M Medal as NRL Player of the Year.

Any tribute to Slater will acknowledge his lightning speed, the amount of ground he covers in each match, his awareness of when to chime into an attack and the fact he has saved almost as many tries as he has scored.

But the one moment that stands out for me was the determination Slater showed to overcome what was initially diagnosed as a tournament-ending knee injury in the quarter final of the 2013 World Cup and play a starring role for Australia in the final at Old Trafford.

Most players would have just accepted their fate after seeing the way the swelling in Slater's left knee ballooned immediately after being taken from the Racecourse Oval in Wales during the match against the USA just two weeks earlier.

Kangaroos' physiotherapist Tony Ayoub later described Slater's efforts to not only play—but star—in Australia's 34–2 win over New Zealand as the most satisfying moment in more than twenty years of working with club and representative teams.

Australian, Queensland and Melbourne captain Cameron Smith labelled it the best performance of his longtime teammate's illustrious career, which until then had included winning grand finals, State of Origin series and Four Nations tournaments but not a World Cup.

Slater's performance and the Kangaroos' triumph enabled the then thirty-year-old to avenge the demons that had haunted him since gifting the winning try to Kiwis playmaker Benji Marshall in the 2008 RLWC decider at Suncorp Stadium.

While he had bristled at questions throughout the tournament about that incident being motivation for success in the UK, Slater admitted afterwards that he did not really know if he would last the match but had been so desperate to play he had worked around the clock to be fit.

For a week leading up to Australia's semifinal at Wembley Stadium, Slater barely ventured outside the Royal Gardens hotel on Kensington High Street, where the team was based, as he iced his knee and underwent treatment from Ayoub.

In fact, Slater barely left his room as he was hooked up to an ice and compression machine for up to eight hours per day.

Yet with just one light training session under his belt before the final, Slater scored 2 tries in a stunning performance he declared was in the top five of his career.

He later underwent surgery that delayed his start to the 2014 season for the Storm.

Because of his brilliance in attack and uncanny ability to read the play in defence, Slater's toughness is often overlooked, but those other attributes that make him such a great player have also made him a target for opposition teams.

To stop Slater wreaking havoc from kick returns, defenders regularly try to smash him as he receives the ball and he has suffered numerous injuries this way, but bravely tries to hide any pain on the field.

Slater, whose weight has never been more than 90 kg, has had to put up with the tactic for much of his career. It resulted in him suffering a knee injury in the second match of the 2012 Origin series that caused him to miss the series decider and troubled him for the remainder of the season and beyond, before eventually threatening his World Cup dream.

Only a special player like Slater could have continued with such an injury for so long, and played so well, that few knew he was troubled by it all.

During that time Slater helped Melbourne to victory over Canterbury in the 2012 grand final and set new records for the most tries by any fullback in premiership history and by a Storm player.

At the same time he has held off challengers for his No 1 jersey in Australian and Queensland teams from two of the best players in the game—Greg Inglis and Jarryd Hayne, who were forced into the centres during the Kangaroos 2013 World Cup campaign.

While it is hard to compare players of different eras, Slater is not just the best fullback but one of the best players I have seen in my time covering the game since 1994—and arguably the toughest.

Brad Walter has covered rugby league for more than twenty years and is the senior league writer for *The Sydney Morning Herald*.

CHAPTER ONE

WILD & CHEEKY

Billy Slater was born to be wild.

Raised in the tropics of Far North Queensland, he grew up with the sometimes dangerous seasons that swung from summer deluges and the threat of cyclones to months of glorious sunshine. It is a landscape that can't be tamed, a place where kids have boundless choices to expend their energy, where kids are strong and full of zest and play on every bit of dry ground they can find. It was a tropical playground for a young Billy who loved swimming, snorkelling, diving and fishing.

The Slaters were battlers. Ronnie, Billy's dad, drove trucks taking bananas from farms down to the depot in Innisfail for distribution, while his mum, Judy, a top touch football player, was skilled at packing bananas in record time. They lived on the outskirts of town in Innisfail in a place known as Goondi Bend, where the Bruce Highway does an awkward

S-turn. It was here, not far from the racetrack, Billy would forge friendships for life. They'd play together, go to primary school at Goondi State School and then head off to Innisfail High School.

Billy was as energetic and cheeky as kids come. The larrikin streak came from his dad, Ronnie, known everywhere as 'Mophead' because of his large mop of hair. Billy added to the tough Slater profile with his wide open smile and his ability to run fast.

In his teenage years Billy was always out skylarking and playing football out on a friend's front yard or in the street in the close where he lived. His mates used to get one of his uncles to drive them up to Mena Creek for a swim, or they'd head off to Josephine Falls to swim amongst the huge river boulders and dangerous currents. Billy was renowned for surfing down the slippery big rock shelf in his bare feet as the water skimmed over the top, showing off his amazing centre of balance. Billy and his mates also loved jumping off the Kalbo railway bridge into the South Johnstone River. Billy could do a forward flip then a back flip before hitting the water.

His mate Mark Averkoff said Billy rarely had a ball out of his hand. 'He was always one of the smaller kids, and he loved the kick and chase, eh.'

Billy, when playing down on the grass at Goondi Bend, was often told by the other players 'you're too small, go off to the wing Billy!'

Billy's cousin James, who lived in East Innisfail, agrees that Billy always had a football in his hand: 'During school, after school, in the rain and in the floods. He just loved it.'

Averkoff would cycle 4 km on tracks through the middle of cane fields to meet up with Billy. 'We were always playing football and basketball down the park.' They went on larks to the Falls, jumping off bridges, and later when someone in the crew got old enough to drive, they went down to Etty Bay for a late night sea swim.

'He was proper cheeky, always had someone chasing him. He had to learn to be fast. He was always funny, always laughing,' Averkoff said. Billy loved a laugh. But he had bounds. While others would take a joke too far, Billy knew when to reel it in.

Sometimes Billy gave the appearance of a kid at a loose end, disinterested in school, where he often said he just went to 'eat his lunch'. His career ambition was to drive a truck like his day. As a teen, he was often seen getting around town in a T-shirt emblazoned with 'blood, sweat and beers'. It said a lot about his sense of fun. But deep inside there was respect and a determination to succeed; a 'want' his friends saw in him, and a work ethic that would drive him to success.

Billy played rugby league for the Brothers team in Innisfail, but he became disillusioned with the sport. He was smallish and got pummelled in tackling. He didn't make a junior representative side and it looked like he was better at tennis than rugby league.

At the age of thirteen Billy thought he could be a jockey—Ronnie and Billy loved the horses, riding them and following them at the races. Pease Park, the Innisfail racetrack, was like a second home. Sick and tired of being behind the pace in his team, Billy hung up his boots and turned his attention solely to horses. Billy urged his dad to get him a spot working part-time in a local training stable. There weren't that many to choose from in Innisfail and it was only natural their friends, the Stricklands, would oblige. Greg Strickland's kids grew up with Billy at Goondi Bend and they shared a love of sport and of horses. Billy and Strickland's eldest son Beau were great mates, although sometimes they were known to chase one another up the street after a heated encounter, usually a row about football.

Racing and having a bet is as normal as playing rugby league in the Far North. It has produced some of the best horse trainers in the land—Brian Mayfield-Smith, the trainer who finally ended Tommy Smith's historic run of Sydney training premierships, and John O'Shea, who after a stellar career in Sydney was appointed the lead trainer in Australia for the international Darley operation. Racing was one of the ways people socialised in the Far North, especially at meetings known as the Annuals.

Billy started at the stables where all stablehands start—at the bottom with the menial duties of mucking out stables, carting water and filling feed bins. But Billy got to spend a lot of time with horses, which he loved. Strickland quickly saw his ability on a horse and it wasn't long before Billy was also doing track work with some of Strickland's best horses.

Strickland once saw him ride a horse six or seven times around Innisfail's Pease Park almost at full gallop. 'After he stopped, he stood high in the stirrups and looked at his watch to see how fast he'd gone,' Strickland said.

Strickland found a nice thoroughbred for Billy that had raced under the name Munchin' Away. Billy bought the horse for a carton of beer and renamed it Whisky and rode it around and around the training track at Pease Park. He eventually turned Whisky into a good jumper, and Slater and Whisky competed in show jumping events for the Innisfail Pony Club.

They won several regional gymkhana ribbons. Pony Club member Stacey Locastro remembers Billy as 'quiet, but cheeky'. She said he was quite a sight in his younger days, arriving at pony club riding Whisky bareback from home like an American Indian. Stacey was amazed one day when she saw Billy and a friend riding upside down on their horses at the Mareeba Show. 'Billy was always laughing, always winning, but always very humble,' Stacey said.

In his first year at pony club, Whisky won the title of most improved horse (now the trophy is known as the Billy Slater Trophy, the most prestigious and hard-fought for title at the Innisfail Pony Club). Billy won many gymkhana events from barrel racing to novelty races and show jumping. (Billy didn't forget his pony club friends when he entered the big time, sending a signed shirt and his football boots from Melbourne for a fundraising event to help Stacey's daughter compete at the Queensland dressage titles.)

As his family weren't that well-off Billy often had to hitch a ride for himself and Whisky on his friends' horse floats to the gymkhanas up to the Tablelands. Fatefully, during his gymkhana days, he met a smiling, vivacious Nicole Rose on the jumping circuit. They used to get around as great mates with no inkling that it might later lead to a life together. Nicole was from Cairns and she knew nothing about rugby league, but they shared a love of horses.

By the time Billy sold Whisky she was worth $2000—about fifty cartons of beer. Stacey ended up with her in her paddock, but Whisky refused to obey anyone but Billy. She was the most sought-after horse in the club.

Billy kept up his schooling at Innisfail High School even though he hated it. He spent all his spare time around horses and the stables. Strickland observed Billy's physical change as he handled more and more thoroughbreds. Strickland and Ronnie believe it was the track work that turned Billy from a gangly small kid into a strong muscle-bound athlete. The downside to Billy's growth spurt was that his weight meant he would never realise his dream to be a jockey.

Strickland set Billy a challenge one day at the stables. 'See that bucket, bet you can't pick it up with one hand.' It was a four gallon bucket that weighed more than 20 kg. Billy had a go, but all he got for trying the feat as he carried it between his legs was water splashing all the way down into his gumboots.

'About a year later, when he was fourteen or so, he came and said, "Hey Stricky, look at this" and he picked the bucket up with one hand. I said "good, now your next challenge is to do this"'. Strickland knelt down and picked the bucket up with one finger. 'Billy was always up for a challenge, I think that was his inner fire, loving a challenge.'

Billy continued to play touch football, along with surfing, diving and spearfishing, but there was no indication of the amazing footballer to follow. Billy's older sister Sheena was, like their mum, a top touch football player. Sheena joined in the football games in the backyard, especially at their friends' the Westeras' house, where Sheena was friends with Tarah Westera. Tarah was surprised when Billy rose from his humble start to become the giant footballer of his generation, going on what she'd seen in backyards. 'Billy was never a good player at school. His dad coached, but Billy just wasn't a football player, he just did his horse stuff. We'd all play together in the backyard and with Sheena.' Tarah would become a league player and would later play for the Australian women's league team, the Jillaroos.

Billy was struggling with his football while his mates, including Beau Strickland, went off for representative duties for Queensland. But Beau, who was two years older than Billy, saw plenty of potential in him while others didn't. He had enough faith in Billy's ability to urge selectors to put him in the under-18s squad for Innisfail Brothers when Billy was sixteen. It was the unlikely start that would help propel Billy into the big time.

Billy took on his role with gusto even though he was the youngest in the side by far. The Innisfail side slowly climbed the ladder and made the regional grand final against Atherton.

Beau was a big prop forward and looked after his smaller Goondi mate Billy. No-one could believe their eyes when the slight Billy ran through the pack in the grand final and was tackled just short of the line. After the next play, Billy took the ball at dummy half, made a great fake pass and scored under the posts. It wasn't quite good enough though, as Atherton went on to win the grand final. (Playing against Billy in the Atherton side was a young Dallas Johnson, who would go on to play alongside and debut with Billy at the Melbourne Storm and also represent Australia. The northern competition was brimming with talent.)

Beau remembers in one game in the under-18s Billy was ruffled by the ref's decision. The referee was someone he once played with down on the grass verges at Goondi Bend. 'Billy puffed his chest up big-time and wasn't going to take no for an answer. He was kind of thinking "I'll take you on,"' remembers Beau.

'Billy had a tough skin, I know, because we often used to chase each other up the street. He was pretty fiery. He was also a cheeky bugger, he was always cheeky.' When upset, Billy was renowned for throwing the football at an opposition player.

'Billy had persistence. He just kept pushing, pushing and pushing. He always had this talent and we always had this belief in him,' Beau said. 'It was amazing, he talked, he stood up and he became the leader, he knew all the positions and plays way before all the other players. He was always one or two steps ahead of everyone else.'

Beau said, although the Slaters were renowned for toughness, they were a great bunch of people. Beau would often take Billy up to the Brothers club for a game of pool and buy him a coke to chill out after a game. He never got over how much Billy changed physically, riding track work for his dad, and then, suddenly had this amazing growth spurt.

Billy also had a breakthrough, winning a representative spot in a combined Innisfail–Eacham side. Selector Darren Blooranta put his trust in the raw talent of Billy as a sixteen-year-old. It was Billy's first representative jumper.

'That kicked him off,' Ronnie Slater told *The Cairns Post*. 'He was always the little fella. He always had the skill and was a tricky bugger but could never make a rep side. I remember they [the rep side] were after players and a few of them had pulled out. They rang and said "does Billy want a run in the rep side?" Billy said "yes" straight away.'

Darren Blooranta told *The Cairns Post*:

> I could just see he had the raw talent. I could see it straight away. I always wondered why he was missed. He was just a great kid. He was just good with his hands on the ball. I just knew he had that ability to go further. He had that speed and manoeuvrability. I don't take any accolades for anything he has achieved, but just to say I was associated with him is a big deal for me.

But Billy's league breakthrough was short-lived and he had run out of patience for school. Out of nowhere came an incredible offer to work at one of Australia's most famous racing stables. A female track rider from Strickland's stable had won an apprenticeship at Gai Waterhouse's stables at Randwick in Sydney.

Strickland took a call from the foreman at Tulloch Lodge. 'Got any more good riders up there?' Strickland said he had a young kid who was as keen as mustard and had great hands for a horse. It was, of course, Billy.

Billy was about to be jettisoned into the big smoke from an outback town. He'd hardly seen Brisbane when he was about to land in the biggest city in Australia. His mum Judy helped pack his bags and travelled down with him to Sydney when all the arrangements had been sorted out.

But at the back of Billy's mind was always the thought he could make it in the league. It kept gnawing at him. After all, he'd just won that rep jumper.

Billy eked out his last days at Innisfail High School without any desire for studying. Later in life he'd say he had only read two books in his life. One day, teacher's aide Mrs Rosa Binello walked into his high school class to check on things. Billy was at the back of the class, swinging on a chair.

'What are you doing Billy, when are you going to start learning?' she challenged him. 'If you want to drive a truck like your dad you'll have to sit for a licence and you'll have to study for that. You have to learn stuff or you'll never get a job.'

Billy, with his big smile, cut back: 'I don't have to learn Mrs Binello, I'm going to play footy for Australia one day.'

CHAPTER TWO

PAELLAS, POTATOES & FOOTY

The forebears of Billy Slater were tough and resilient people who forged their futures and fame with their bare hands by cane farming or in the boxing ring. They stepped into the Far North's ever-changing wild and wet land early last century, part of an exotic mix of Spanish and Irish migrants who took to farming on the rich volcanic soils.

Billy's family links run rich in Spanish blood on one side of his family. Billy's grandmother, his father Ronnie's mother, was Connie Astorquia, the daughter of a Spanish migrant, Juan, from the Basque area of Spain. It was a twist of fate that brought Juan to Australia, and if people look for a sign to Billy's fleet-footedness they need look no further than to the exploits of his great-grandfather.

The Astorquias were simple sheep farmers in the foothills of the Pyrenees in the Basque region of northern Spain. Juan's mother had died suddenly after the birth of her last child. Juan's father, Adrien, sought ways to get by and sent his eldest son to America to earn money for the family. The remaining brothers were urged to leave their village of Aulestia, in the region of Biskaia, at a time when civil unrest was bubbling in Spain and as the youths faced possible conscription into the military reserve to fight in Morocco.

Juan and two brothers travelled to nearby France. Juan wanted to immigrate to America, and needing the money, entered a foot race, which he won, giving him the money for his ticket to a new life. It was pot luck that he ended up in Australia. In 1913, while he was foot racing, his brothers left on a boat for America. Juan missed it and took the next boat out of France—and this one was heading for Australia. It was entirely accidental and it took another generation before family links were restored. He was leaving for a place he had never heard of, with people he didn't know, at the age of fifteen. The boat, the German steamship *Seydlitz*, was full of many Spaniards who were immigrating to the various countries the ship called into. On the way to his new homeland Juan met his future wife Connie (senior), who was migrating from the Catalan area of Spain, where her family owned a cork factory.

In the early 1900s, land was easily accessible in the Far North for migrants willing to put in the hard work of establishing and running sugar cane farms with all the seasonal variants. Juan arrived in Brisbane in July 1913 and later travelled up to the Far North to work on the railway from Cairns to Kuranda along the wild Barron River. It took a long time for him to get established. Juan kept in touch with Connie and eventually invited her to join him in South Johnstone, just west of Innisfail. He started a market garden and then turned to sugar cane farming with other Spanish migrants who saw its great potential. An active, tall, slight man with a thick crop of hair, his family eked out a living in the land of extremes in a life built around sugar cane.

Juan did a lot of his work by hand, clearing rainforest for his cane plantations. He would plant the cane stalks amid the stumps of the newly cleared forest and they would later blow up the stumps one by one. To build his house he placed huge round timber logs deep in the ground and sawed it off from the top to complete the frame for an original pole home. Everything was still frontier land in the 1920s and the cut cane was carried by horse out from the fields. In December 1925, he declared in an advertisement in *The Cairns Post* his desire to become an Australian citizen.

Juan was friends with many other Spanish migrants who had settled in the area including José Paronella, who travelled on the *Seydlitz* with him to Australia. They established cane farms and on-sold them. Later, Juan helped José find land out near Mena Creek, where Paronella eventually built an amazing rainforest retreat known as Paronella Park (now one of Queensland's top tourist attractions).

Using reinforced concrete, Paronella spent six years building the maze of balustrades, tunnels, secret paths, swimming pools, recreation areas and a ballroom. He even built a hydro-electric operation running off the rushing waters of Mena Creek. In the ballroom, an amazing mirror ball with nearly 1300 mirrors reflected light all around the room. There was a tennis court and people enjoyed dances, parties and wedding receptions. He established a grand arcade of kauri pines and built a bamboo forest by the creek as border against the neighbouring farmland. It was an oasis of fun, rest and pleasure in the 1930s.

Juan was a keen surfer and helped build the surf club at Etty Bay. Some of the markings on the club mimic exactly the decorations used at Paronella Park. All the Astorquias loved the water and were often involved in rescuing people. Juan's son Ron rescued two people who had fallen in the river and his younger son Adrian saved a swimmer at Etty Bay. Juan was also a top lawn bowler and both he and Connie won ribbons around Australia in lawn bowls. Juan also practised the Basque tradition of stone lifting with his Spanish friends. The rural heritage and sports of the Basque country perfectly fitted in with the life on the plains and farmland surrounding Innisfail.

The young people of the cane fields in the thirties and forties met up at the Saturday night dances either at the Innisfail Show Hall, the Mourilyan Hall or the Palmerston School.

His son Ron's wife Julie, of Irish extraction, said the seasons were divided between rugby league in the winter and surf club activities in the summer. 'Wherever we were during the year, we'd put a blanket down and run around.'

League was the dominant sport in the Far North from the early 1920s. 'In those days you could drive your car into the grounds and watch a game from there,' said Julie. Julie watched as rugby league outshone any other traditions the Astorquias might have kept from Spain. 'All the Storkys played league, the whole lot of them, I can't think of one that didn't,' declares Julie. (Many male Astorquias were nicknamed Stork).

On the other side of Billy's family were the Irish Slaters, who were also involved in the cane industry. When Juan's daughter Connie Astorquia married William Slater, Billy's grandfather, they held their reception in the ballroom of Paronella Park.

William, also known as Bill, (Billy would be named after him) was a cane inspector and the family grew up in South Johnstone. It was a hard life and there were no more down-to-earth people than the Slaters. Connie would live in South Johnstone most of her married life.

Mena Creek was the playground for Bill and Connie's progeny—three boys, all of whom would go on to play rugby league at regional cup level. They were all full of spirit and great larrikins. Billy's dad, Ronnie, had no trepidation in diving straight off the rock face at Mena Creek, a fall of 50 feet into the bubbling milky pool. The pool now carries warning signs of crocodiles in the area, but back then in the 1950s, Ronnie attests, it was free of big crocs.

'Now you wouldn't put your toe in it,' said Ronnie. 'We used to run the show there [at Paronella Park].'

The young Slaters would run through Paronella Park, scampering through the long tunnels and hiding in the vast stands of bamboo and rainforest.

Billy's grandfather, Bill, whose nickname was 'Wedgehead', was a top boxer and fought at the bantamweight level. When he started learning boxing he went to the boxing trainer as a southpaw, but the trainer turned him into an orthodox and the move worked. Bill could hold his ground to anyone silly enough to take him on. He was often mentioned in the boxing columns of the Far North's newspapers when boxing pulled big crowds. In May 1951 at Pease Park, Bill, hailed as the 'local champion', knocked out a boxer from the famed Jimmy Sharman boxing tent inside sixty seconds of the first round as 300 parochial fans cheered on.

Later on, Bill was urged to come out of retirement for a special bout with the welterweight champion of Queensland, Lou Ballico, of Mareeba, who once fought for an Australian title. No-one wanted to take on the champ and he needed a warm-up bout before his next match. Bill boldly told all and sundry: 'I'll take him on'. If the expression punching above your weight meant anything, it applied to Bill that night when he stepped into the ring, giving away almost a stone of weight to his formidable opponent. Bill fought at about 8 stone, 6 lbs. The bout in the Innisfail Show Hall pulled a huge crowd with the pundits expecting Bill to take an early exit. But he fought famously through several rounds before losing to Ballico.

Bill also knew how to ride a horse, and later took young Billy out riding, instilling the love of horses in him.

The Slater brothers—Tommy (Snake), Johnny (no nickname, although according to Tommy, he 'was called a few names but was ready to set someone straight if they called him a bad one') and Ronnie (Mophead)—were all good runners, footballers and boxers. Johnny wanted to be a jockey but weight foiled his ambition. Connie was also a very fast runner.

Connie's Spanish roots were quickly absorbed into the Irish–Australian heritage and Ronnie only remembers eating 'Aussie fare', such as bacon and eggs, and potatoes at home. But Tommy said she cooked a lot of 'that Spanish stuff' with rice and seafood.

Ronnie said the meeting of half-Irish and half-Spanish blood was a 'dangerous mix'. Ronnie was fearless in his tackling when playing league. Through his whole career he had to fight niggling knee injuries but he became a top player at regional level. As Billy eventually became an all-round athlete, so Ronnie's generation was always active. 'We were all athletes, lifesavers,' Ronnie said.

It seemed inevitable that Ronnie would somehow become involved in the cane industry, where, he said, there was 'always plenty of money'. His first job was working at the South Johnstone sugar mill and then later driving cane trains or binning in the field during cane harvesting, which sometimes went on for six or seven months right up until Christmas. Later he would get involved in the other big industry in the Far North—bananas.

However, rugby league was in their blood. Ronnie's uncle Adrian was the first Astorquia to hit the big time, playing for Innisfail and North Queensland before a stint with Manly in Sydney. Ronnie and his brothers Tommy and Johnny all became top Queensland club league players and coaches.

The Slater brothers played in the great era of the Foley Shield, a challenge cup that started in 1948 and was the Holy Grail for the league faithful in the Far North. There is hardly an Astorquia or Slater male that hasn't played Foley Shield football. Bill played for Suburbs in Innisfail, and then for Innisfail in the Foley Shield, as a hooker. The Shield was an inter-town competition that brought Far North teams together from Mt Isa down to Townsville. Under the Shield's rules, the grand final was always played in Townsville, to honour the memory of Townsville's Arch Foley, a pioneer of rugby league in the Far North. Towns played in a round robin competition amongst three groups before they earned the right to play off for the Shield in Townsville. Every town followed the Foley games with unbridled fervour. It was the breeding ground for many Kangaroo players and was the launch pad for many top flight league careers. It was also the grounding for the Slater brothers, and the inspiration and enthusiasm it created was passed down the line to Billy.

According to his cousin Sue Astorquia, Ronnie developed an uncanny ability to jump up high as a young boy, a trait inherited by Billy. 'I remember as a kid watching him do three somersaults in the air. He started off with one, then two and eventually just made the third,' Sue said. 'There were lots of ground thumps between doing two and learning to do three.'

Ronnie was always nimble on his feet and in his career was caught between being a lock and a five-eighth. His playing mate Mick Quinn remembers Ronnie was just not quite big enough for a lock, and just a bit big for a five-eighth. But one thing Ronnie never lacked was confidence on the field.

Rugby league was still wild and woolly and on-field fights were common and mostly went unpunished. Quinn said when Ronnie coached Brothers he was 'like a breath of fresh air. He challenged and encouraged all the players and they responded. For Ronnie it was tough because he was always trying to get over troublesome knee injuries'.

Quinn said:

> When we were growing up, Foley Shield was the pinnacle. We had some great players up on the Tablelands and that's what every rugby league player aspired to get to [the Foley Shield]. Some went on to play for Australia and their dreams came true. When you think what someone like Kerry Boustead did, it's a genuine achievement. Any strong Foley Shield player could have got a position with a first-grade Brisbane club.

Ronnie said league was the only sport people followed. 'It was the only thing we did. We played Foley on a Sunday and all your mates played. Aussie Rules never existed.'

Ronnie's league career would take him around the state of Queensland. Ronnie helped secure a Foley Shield victory for Innisfail in 1975 after losing the closely fought 1973 Foley final against Whitsunday. For a short while he went down to Brisbane and tried the big league in Brisbane, playing for Redcliffe in 1977, before returning north. He then won a second Shield while playing for Mt Isa in 1979. Ronnie played rugby league for Southern Suburbs in Innisfail. At one stage they had four sides in the local competition—Southern Suburbs, Brothers, Babinda and Uniteds.

His brother Tommy has mixed recollections of the Foley Shield battles. He would have played in the 1975 Foley Shield final but suffered a broken jaw in an on-field incident at a lead-up game while playing for his Innisfail club side Suburbs against Uniteds, coached by his uncle Adrian. Tommy went down heavily on the ground but many were unsure if he'd been hit with a knee or a flying fist. He had dirt all over his face when he got up off the ground and his jaw was shattered. Tommy said he's still not sure who the rogue player was who delivered the brutal hit, but some in Innisfail believe they know the culprit. Tommy played at five-eighth after moving from the centres because 'I lost a bit of speed'.

'These were great days [in the 1970s] when you could play for Australia from any club in Australia, from Mareeba, from anywhere; now you have to go through the NRL,' Tommy said.

Before Innisfail's big 1975 victory in the Foley Shield, Innisfail had to play Eacham for a place in the final and won by three points, right on the bell. (Eacham was an amalgamation of teams from up on the Atherton Tablelands.) Graham Bevan, who played for Wests in Sydney in his first class career, was in the Eacham side. Tommy reckons Eacham would have beaten Townsville too in the final if they'd got through. 'They were a good side [Eacham],' said Tommy.

Johnny Slater, who was a very fast player, also played in two Foley Shield finals, winning one of them. He was forced to give up league after he kept getting black spots in his eyes, believed to be the result of concussion injuries he incurred over his football years. According to Tommy, a doctor warned him he could go blind if he kept playing.

Vince Cooper, a rugged canecutter, played at prop alongside Ronnie for much of the late 70s and was there when Ronnie 'played a blinder' to help defeat Townsville 15–4 to win the Foley Shield in 1975. Ronnie's uncle Adrian Astorquia was the Innisfail coach. 'Ronnie should have been a halfback but he wasn't small enough. For some reason he always wanted to be a forward. He had beautiful hands and he was really good at backing up. He was good at breaking the line too.'

Ronnie was suffering as the final in Townsville approached. He had a serious groin strain and took a handful of Dencorub and lathered himself in ointment. He somehow managed to last through to the seventieth minute of the game. Innisfail won the final. One of the players was Ian Boustead, the brother of international sensation Kerry Boustead. Ian Boustead would go on to a league career in Brisbane. Another Innisfail player, Nick Nicollo, went on to play for Easts in Brisbane.

The Innisfail crowd went mad at their victory—only their fourth in the history of the Shield—but there was a hitch to the celebrations. When the Innisfail team went to check out of their motel the next morning in Townsville they found they didn't have enough money to pay. Stepping into the breach was a local businessman whose last name was Dodge, who made up the shortfall. Innisfailians always recount how they got out of Townsville in the 1975 Foley final thanks to a 'Dodgey cheque'. If they were really stuck for money they might have turned to someone linked closely to their back-up crew, who acted also as a bookmaker and won thousands of dollars on the game. Townsville were doubly dejected because they had backed themselves considerably to win the final. Betting was common on the Foley matches. The players received a small $20 bonus for winning the Shield. On their return to Innisfail, the jubilant players ended up at the Queens Hotel to drink the night away after their famous victory. The celebrations went on for a week.

It was the last Foley Shield victory for Innisfail in their own right, later teaming up with Eacham to win three more Foley Shields.

After his great performances at the top of Far North football, Ronnie was given the honour of representing North Queensland. Ronnie continued his league career in Mt Isa, the tough outback mining centre where if you didn't work you weren't trying. He joined the Townies Club as a lock and enjoyed the heyday of league in the mining town when league players were feted like royalty. The Townies had numerous sponsors and when they had to play in Townsville they were flown down there and put up at a top motel for the night before flying home. The Mt Isa team had strappers and an assortment of managers.

In this idyllic situation it was not surprising Ronnie fell in love. Ronnie met Judy Simonsen at one of the regular league social functions. Judy was the attractive daughter of Noel Simonsen, a well-known referee both in the district and in regional Queensland. (Noel was also a country music singer who toured regional Queensland. Billy was sometimes seen hopping up on stage with his grandad in a cowboy hat to play guitar, especially when Pop called in to the Goondi hotel.) They settled down very quickly to start a new life together and had their first child, Sheena. Judy was a top runner herself, competing in many athletics carnivals. Their kids were destined to be speedy.

Ronnie would sometimes joke about marrying a top line runner in Judy. Someone once asked him 'I heard your missus was a sprinter?'

Ronnie replied 'Yeah, but she wasn't fast enough—I caught her.'

Ronnie was in the prime of his life. His upper body was finely muscled and often on show in tight-fitting T-shirts—one even carried the slogan 'You can count on a Queenslander'. He was ready to take on any formidable opponent. He sported a big moustache and had a smile as wide as the land.

Steve Bax played with Ronnie in the late 70s and remembered he was 'a little grubby' when it came to tackling, not afraid to put the knee in to an opposition player. 'Ronnie was in your face all the time,' he said. 'He showed a keenness to take on anyone who wanted to argue about a point on the field', said Bax. Bax reckons Billy inherited some of that niggle when he first started playing but soon learned to give that style of tackling away. Bax reckons Billy's speed came more from his mum's bloodlines. Judy was 'fast' on the athletics field.

Despite being isolated in the hot dry outback of Queensland, Mt Isa had one of the best football playing surfaces of any northern town. The only thing visiting players would complain about was the smell of the smoke drifting over from the mining smelter.

Such was the following for football, Mt Isa supported four football clubs, from which the Mt Isa Foley Shield side was chosen. Up to 3000 people would turn up for a game, especially if it was a Foley Shield fixture.

'In those days we were treated like kings. Anyone who didn't have a job got one through Norm's Electrics, who always looked after the players. Most of us worked out on the mine projects. Norm never minded if you were late on a Monday after a big weekend of footy,' said Bax.

When Ronnie went back to Mt Isa in the 1990s to a reunion, he brought a young Billy with him. Bax remembers playing touch and watching this kid 'run 100 miles an hour' down the sideline.

'I said: "Whose boy's that?" and someone said "Ronnie's"'.

'When I see Billy play, I often see a bit of Ronnie in him.'

Through the Mt Isa club president, Ronnie accepted an offer to play for Maroochydore and moved his family down to Nambour. Judy also had family in the area. On 18 June 1983, Judy gave birth to a bright, bouncing boy they simply named Billy (not a shortening of William). Billy grew up in a house full of league talk with Ronnie at the crest of his career. Wherever he went on the Sunshine Coast, Ronnie created memories that people still talk about today.

Former player James Ward, now chief executive of the Sunshine Coast Rugby League Club, can recall seeing 'Mophead' run in some strong performances on the coast:

I remember playing against Ronnie 'Mophead' Slater when he was playing for Maroochydore. I can remember when in the twilight of his playing days that Mophead was asked to help out the rep team [the Sunshine Coast] because there were a number of players unavailable, and the team was young and inexperienced. He was a lock, but played five-eighth in this particular game at the Nambour Showground, a match that he almost single-handedly took control of to see the Coast win.

Benny Pike, who also played for Townie's club in Mt Isa, saw Ronnie on the field: 'Ron was a fantastic player and great bloke.'

Player Steve Molineux remembers the larrikin side of Ronnie and how his skills brought success to Maroochydore:

He played at Maroochydore in the 82 grand final side and the 83 premiership side—Maroochydore's first premiership. I do remember bouncing Billy on my knee at a few of Mophead's legendary barbecues. He also played rep footy for Wide Bay and Sunshine Coast in 83 and 84. He was captain of the 84 Wide Bay side when we played Great Britain at Bundaberg's Slater Park [no connection].

Mophead was, and still is, one of funniest buggers you would ever meet. Disrespectful, terrible trainer, loved a beer, but shit he could play footy.

Ronnie left Maroochydore after the 83 premiership to captain–coach Noosa for two years in 84 and 85.

Nick Webster, who played with Ron at Noosa, remembers a huge stink in 1985 when Noosa walked off the field after Ronnie was given his marching orders by the referee. 'In 85 we were playing Beerwah, Bill Hourigan was the ref. After the penalty count got ridiculous Ron went up and questioned him and he gave Ron ten minutes, so we all left the field in protest. They gave us five minutes to return but we would not return without Ron. The match was a forfeit. It caused a big stir back then.'

Tommy Slater had also played in southern Queensland. He played at Souths in 1978 and 1979 and for the Sunshine Coast's 47th Battalion winning sides of those two years. He also coached Kingaroy and only just lost a final when taking on the Cleal Brothers, Noel and Les, who were playing for Wondai, in the South Burnett competition final of 1976.

Ronnie retired after the 1985 season at Noosa and the Slater family returned to Innisfail and a new life at Goondi Bend.

* * *

By the age of six Billy had made his debut as a junior on the rugby league field at Innisfail when he was given the chance to play in the under-8s in a Saturday club competition. It was a friendly competition put together by the local clubs on a Saturday morning.

Mick Quinn remembers the young Slater starting on the field when Mick was overseeing the under-8s comp in Innisfail. 'He was a tiny little fellow but just got involved in it as much as he could. We had him at dummy half so we looked after him. You wouldn't say he was a tackler, anyway at that age it was all about fun.'

The men who played Foley Shield, including Mick and Ronnie, watched on as the next generation of footballers started off. At that stage football was something to keep them busy and great exercise, and when the kids fell over, a bit of a laugh. Neither of them knew how far little Billy would go in the game.

CHAPTER THREE

BILLY ON TRACK

Billy hit his straps at the age of sixteen but not in the way he expected. The straps were those tied about horses and he was about to be let loose into the hustle and bustle of a big city and one of Australia's most famous racing stables. Weighing just 65 kg, he was put in charge of 500 kg highly-strung racehorses, some of them worth millions of dollars.

Tulloch Lodge was a place where legends were made. Tommy (TJ) Smith and his brothers had started the operation in the 1940s. They turned a cantankerous buckjumper called Bragger into a major city race winner. The small fortune they won from backing Bragger gave them the seed money to create one of the most phenomenal training establishments in the country. TJ eventually trained two of the greatest champions of the Australian turf—Tulloch and Kingston Town. At one time in his illustrious career, TJ was nominated as the best horse trainer in the world. He won thirty-three Sydney training premierships in a row until a North Queenslander (Brian Mayfield-Smith) knocked him briefly off his pedestal. TJ's only child, Gai, picked up the reins of the operation in her father's later years, after gaining a training licence in 1992, and when Billy arrived she was achieving her own amazing milestones in the racing game.

Billy's mum, Judy, travelled down to Sydney from Innisfail with Billy when he started his new life at Tulloch Lodge. Many of the employees were horse-wise English and Irish backpackers moving through Australia on holidays. It was a high-powered business with Gai putting her eye over every minute part of the stable.

Billy was in the oldest digs for stable hands, living across the road from the main stables, in Bowral Street, just off Randwick racecourse. You couldn't swing one of the stable's many cats in Billy's new lodgings—living conditions didn't get more basic. Even his tiny room had been cut in two, with a three-quarter partition down the middle. It wasn't much bigger than the average laundry.

Billy was required to perform all the menial duties of a stable hand. The pressure was on. At times, Judy was so worried about him she would come and stay with him for short periods.

Waterhouse's foreman Pat Sexton oversaw Billy's time at Tulloch Lodge. 'He came down from Innisfail and stayed in the stables. He was a very good rider. He had tremendous hands—just like he has with the football. He had tremendous work ethic, like he does now. He loved a joke and was very confident. But Billy was treated the same as everyone else.'

For the race and horse loving Slaters, being at Tulloch Lodge was like a chocolate lover earning a live-in spot at a chocolate factory.

In the early mornings at track work, Billy was working amongst some of the best riders in the country including Jimmy Cassidy and Shane Dye. Cassidy, nicknamed 'The Pumper', had no idea the young Billy would one day be voted the best footballer in the world and that he would later fly to Melbourne just to watch him play at the Storm. He thought Billy could have made it in racing. 'He might have been a fine jockey,' The Pumper declared.

Sexton always found Billy very approachable and if he needed extra work performed around the stables, Billy was ready to do it. 'He was never any trouble, just a lovely country kid.'

Billy's great uncle Adrian Astorquia, who had moved from Innisfail to play league in Sydney with Manly, looked after Billy on his break from the stables. When he first went to pick up Billy, Gai came rushing out to check out who Adrian was, to make sure he wasn't a stranger. 'Oh, you two look the same, you can go,' she said. Adrian said she was very protective of Billy.

Adrian helped Billy have a good time, taking him to a few Sydney watering holes. Billy, like his dad, had an eye for the horses, always including the numbers one, four, six and nine in his trifecta bets.

Billy also started his love of surfing in Sydney, taking his time out during the day to head down to Maroubra or Coogee for a surf. It would become a lifelong passion.

Jockey Mark Newnham, who would later become Gai's lead foreman, saw the young Billy riding at track work. 'He was like a lot of the young guys who came to the stables, enthusiastic and clearly had a genuine love of racing and of horses. He did everything from mucking out stables, leading out horses and riding track work.'

Newnham said he was shocked a few years later when someone pointed out to him that the young track rider was now playing professional football for the Storm. 'He had plenty of natural ability and plenty of determination.'

Billy, though, soon found the constant early starts for little money hard to take. He had to get up at 3 am, five days a week, to ride track work, muck out stables and groom horses. He was earning just $200 a week, while some of the other riders, most of them backpackers with little knowledge of horses, were getting $400 a week. Although his accommodation was free it was a small space, a room that had been cut in half. A lot of rooms were needed to fit in all the Tulloch Lodge employees.

One day Billy summoned up enough gumption to approach Waterhouse over his wages.

'Because of your age,' she said. 'I can't give you any more, but I tell you what, I'll give you an extra $40 if you mow the lawns.' It seemed like the old business brain of her father TJ Smith was coming out of Gai, ever keen to strike a deal. Billy did the mowing anyway.

Billy was doing it all for the experience. It gave him the opportunity to groom and look after some of the stable stars, including Tempest Morn and the gelding Assertive Lad, which won the Magic Millions as a two-year-old just before

Billy arrived and then, with Billy as strapper, ran third in the Golden Slipper, followed by sensational wins in the Sires Produce and Champagne Stakes.

Billy's stable favourite was a gelding called Domero, a moderate former whose career, unlike Billy's, went backwards. Domero ended his racing life in the bush in Western Australia (at his last start he ran 14 lengths last).

One of the Tulloch foremen, Brett Killian, formed a bond with the young Billy. 'He was a fresh country kid and very obliging.'

Killian could pick a good horse but said he fell well short when it came to picking a good football player. 'I was in charge of the touch footy side amongst all the stables at Randwick and never picked him [Billy] to play. I'm a good judge, aren't I? No-one will ever let me live that down, I only had to be reminded a few years later when he was playing for the Storm.'

After Billy achieved fame and fortune, Killian contacted him to donate some memorabilia for a charity auction. 'By the next day he'd sent me one of his signed Kangaroo jumpers and then later a signed Kangaroo training shirt. I couldn't speak more highly of him.'

Killian believes at the end of his time at Tulloch Lodge, Billy was homesick. 'I think in the end he just wanted to go home. It was big thing for a kid at that stage of his life and after all, he was a Queenslander.'

Billy also became good friends with another leading Sydney trainer John Size during his time at Royal Randwick, riding track work for Size for free, before Size moved on to further success in Hong Kong.

Billy said of his life at Tulloch Lodge at Randwick: 'Gai would always come and say hello to you, and it was something I love, so it wasn't really work. She had two stables in Sydney and had about 100 horses between them. I learned heaps, seeing how the best go about their business. She's there most days, six or seven days a week. We'd have Sundays off, but I would take horses to the races and lead them around.'

For Billy, despite being amongst the best thoroughbreds in the industry, morning track work was wearing thin. His rugby league genie was itching to come out of the bottle again. Deep down, his heart was in league, not racing. He approached Gai again and told her he wanted to go and play rugby league. 'That's fine,' she said. 'We'll fit you in.'

But he told her: 'There's no way I can keep getting up this early and play league.' So Billy packed his bags for Innisfail and left his fledgling racing career after just six months at the famous stables. Some of the contacts he made at Tulloch Lodge would last through his life and would put him in good stead for casual work later on.

Billy wouldn't forget his Tulloch Lodge days. After the Storm won the 2009 Grand Final, Billy and Nicole hopped in a campervan and headed up the coast all the way from Melbourne to Innisfail. Billy stopped in at Tulloch Lodge and used a camcorder to make a record of all the old haunts where he'd worked as a young sixteen-year-old. He signed autographs and said hello to everyone before heading on up the highway.

* * *

Back in Innisfail, he settled into the local league. His skills were blooming and so was his upper body. The hard work at Tulloch Lodge had turned him into a strong-shouldered athlete and he had high endurance and led from the front—like most of Waterhouse's horses.

Everyone noticed the physical change. His cousin James, Tommy's son, was the same age and couldn't believe the new-look Billy. 'When he went away he was this scrawny little guy but when he got back he was strong and heavier and he'd even got taller. He'd had this amazing growth spurt.'

Billy returned to his roots at the Innisfail Brothers team. Billy had to take stock back on his home turf to work out what he really wanted to be. His career ambitions had hit the crossroads and he now chose league as his best step in life. Billy and his cousin James hatched a plan to further their aims the next year when Billy was seventeen.

'I went back to Innisfail and the footy season was three-quarters of the way through. I started playing in the under-18s in the Cairns competition. I played the last quarter of the season and started enjoying my footy again,' Billy once said.

'I was looking to play some first-grade in Innisfail and I was training by myself and with the club and come February 2001, I just had to make a decision—either play up there or go down and have a crack at things down south. I came home from training one day and sat down with my old man, had a chat and basically we decided now was the time to go and have a crack.'

James Slater reckons it was all about finding new horizons away from torrential downpours.

'We just wanted to get out of Innisfail and see how we went,' said James.

They decided to try their chances at Norths Devils in Brisbane. They jumped in Billy's beaten-up maroon-coloured Magna in early 2001 and headed south down highway number one, dreaming of a new life. It was a madcap plan, with no certainty of success. If it came off, it promised great riches: Norths were the feeder club to the Melbourne Storm.

James's dad Tommy, who'd coached regional Queensland teams and played with some of the best, had helped pave the way for the duo. He phoned his mate and fellow Innisfailian Greg Bandiera to help obtain a trial for James and Billy with the Devils' under-19 Colts. Bandiera wasted no time in going to the top for his old mate Tommy—ringing his old playing friend and Queenslander Mark 'Muppet' Murray, a State of Origin hero, and then the Devils' head of coaching. An international himself, Murray was at the top of the coaching game. In 1999 Murray was appointed the coach of the Queensland Rugby League team and he coached the Maroons for the 1999 and 2000 State of Origin series against the cockroaches. He was a former roommate with (Storm kingpin) John Ribot on the Kangaroos 1982 tour. Working alongside Murray was the future Broncos coach Andy 'Hook' Griffin. Murray arranged for the two teenagers to have a run, but he explained in no uncertain terms they'd left their run a bit late.

'I told Greg the last trial game was on Saturday, and he rang me on a Tuesday,' Murray said. 'I didn't think they'd make it down from Innisfail in time.'

The eager duo surprised Murray by their arrival on Thursday, just two days later. Billy and James drove night and day and the pair just had one stop at Gin Gin during the massive trek of almost 1400 km. The pair were asking a lot to be considered for the side as the Colts had been training for months. Billy arrived with little to show in his scrapbook. All that he had to rely on were the recommendations of Bandiera and his father and uncles, with no schoolboy jerseys pinned to his resume, except for the regional representative jumper from the combined Innisfail–Eacham side. Nevertheless, they were slotted in for a trial game on the Saturday.

What many didn't know was that Ronnie had actually made a pitch to get Billy into his old club of Redcliffe before their Norths adventure. Billy almost became a Dolphin not a Devil.

Redcliffe league historian Jon Sloan remembers: 'Ronnie actually phoned our CEO to see if we could accommodate him. He told our CEO that Billy was a half or five-eighth and didn't play anywhere else but at the time we had two local kids who were the Queensland under-17 half and five-eighth so we stuck with them.'

Sloan said: 'I do enjoy reminding our CEO from then what a good judge he is every time Billy stars in a test or Origin match.'

* * *

If it wasn't for Bandiera, it is unlikely both the Slater boys would have got a look in. Bandiera knew the Slaters and

Astorquias inside out. Bandiera had a similar background to the Astorquias—from a migrant family who'd had to work hard to make a living on the land outside Innisfail. Bandiera's father emigrated from Italy and ran a dairy farm near the pretty town of Millaa Millaa on the Atherton Tablelands. Like most migrant families in the Far North, the Bandieras quickly ditched the round ball for an oval Steeden. Bandiera later came to live and play in Innisfail, playing for Southern Suburbs. Almost all the Slaters and Astorquias had gone through Southern Suburbs and Bandiera was great mates with Tommy Slater and Tommy's uncle Adrian Astorquia. Bandiera had only played four first-grade games before he was thrust, at the age of just seventeen, into the heady atmosphere of a Foley Shield final in 1968, playing for Innisfail against Mackay. Innisfail defeated Mackay 22–12 and the celebrations went on for days.

Sitting in the crowd at the Foley Shield final was the Australian league coach Harry Bath. Bath was one of the greatest league players never to play for Australia—having spent much of his career in England, winning plaudits and trophies there, but not in his home country. Bath spied the young Bandiera's potential and urged one of his contacts at the Sydney club Newtown to sign up the rookie. Bandiera had hardly heard of Sydney, let alone Newtown, when the offer came in the mail.

'I had to quickly look up a map to find out where it was. I wasn't even old enough to sign a contract,' Bandiera said. 'Up until then I was just building hot rods and shit, working in the sugar mill, and playing footy for fun on the weekends.'

Bandiera went straight to the city and his career took off, and after Newtown, he played for Easts, including in the 1972 grand final, playing alongside legends Artie Beetson and Ronnie Coote. He finished his first-grade time with Balmain. Bandiera had league contacts throughout the game and later moved into administration for the Gold Coast league team.

* * *

What Bandiera didn't know at the time, in early 2001, was that he had played a big part in getting one of the greatest modern talents on to the main stage. Billy's meteoric rise would almost mimic Bandiera's: a wide-eyed boy from Innisfail suddenly hitting the big time.

Billy lobbed at his mate Paddy Gardner's place at Boondall in Brisbane's north. Gardner was from Innisfail as well, and had only arrived a few months earlier to play in the senior Devils team. Gardner was two years older than Billy but still remembered him playing in their youth down at Goondi Bend in Innisfail. The Gardner and Slater families were friends.

'He was always a tough little character, always played above his weight, always cheeky and laughing at training,' Gardner said.

Billy hit the ground running. It was like the invasion of the Innisfailians at Norths. Billy soon found himself a unit at Clayfield and found work. He worked in various jobs, firstly at Deagon racecourse, then plastering work and then doing a courier run.

Gardner was happy with the company of his old Innisfail mates. Billy even converted him from a tomato sauce lover to a barbecue sauce lover in the few weeks Billy and James were sharing the house. 'Even when we had pizza he'd pile on the barbecue sauce,' Gardner remembers.

Most of Norths Colts had been sweating it out in the humid Brisbane weather for months and had every right to believe that they would be the first selected for the 2001 line-up. Many were Queensland schoolboy players. The Colts' line-up had already been pencilled in and the Innisfail duo faced the almost impossible task of wrangling their way into the team.

When Murray first saw Billy he didn't recognise the future star. 'He wasn't very big and had knobbly knees,' Murray remembers. Given first impressions from the senior Norths coach, the whole adventure appeared a lost cause. Murray was impressed the boys had made such an effort to get to the trial. He felt it said a lot about their character. But Murray wasn't staying around for long and by April he was appointed as the Storm's coach and was off to Melbourne. But he would regularly return to keep a close eye on the Devils' talent pool.

Although both cousins were allowed to train with the squad there seemed little hope of winning a place in the run-on team. Eventually, James decided that with no job prospects, no car and with uncertainty over his position, his best prospects were back in Innisfail. Billy, who had the previous experience of living away from home, later used his racing contacts to get a job. He again strapped and rode horses, this time for Brisbane trainer Myles Plumb, who was enjoying success with his stayer Native Jazz (at one time second-favourite for the Melbourne Cup). Billy had landed on familiar territory.

Billy kept pushing doors at Norths, turning up at training whenever possible. When the players went on long runs, Billy often came first in the road race. Norths decided they had to give him a run and Billy played in the centres, after trialling on the wing. At that stage Billy earned just $50 a game—if the Devils won—and $20 if they lost. Chicken feed for what was awaiting him around the corner. It was riding track work that kept him going, earning him about $500 a week. This was his 'second job'.

Suddenly Billy was surrounded by players who would become his best friends and future Origin and Australian teammates. In this heady mix of players was Cameron Smith and Cooper Cronk. They didn't know it at the time but they were all heading on a fast-track to fame at the Melbourne Storm, Queensland State of Origin selection and Kangaroo glory.

The Devils has been the home of many great players over time including Australian and South Sydney legend Clive Churchill, who captain–coached the team in 1959 after his sterling career. Other great players from its ranks were Elwyn Walters, Steve Calder, Darryl Brohman, John Sattler, Nick Geiger, Mark Graham, John Payne, Steve Bell, Ross Henrick, Greg Conescu, Mark Murray, Paul Khan, Greg Dowling, Steve Walters and Trevor Gillmeister. Even an English rugby league captain Tommy Bishop had been a Devil, taking the team to a 1974 minor premiership in the twilight of his playing career.

When Billy arrived he was surrounded by, or had only just missed playing with, other modern NRL stars including Matt Geyer, Peter Robinson, Steven Bell, Dallas Johnson, Matt King, Greg Inglis and Michael Crocker. Crocker would become one of his best mates and they'd share a love of surfing.

Murray still has to pinch himself thinking of one Colts photo that shows the young Smith, Cronk and Billy sitting alongside each other. Smith was soon out of Colts and playing Queensland Cup.

A number of people who knew of Billy went to see him train with the Devils. They noticed his athletic build had changed. It was like they all knew something special was about to happen and they didn't want to miss the ride.

Mick Quinn, the man who'd played Foley Shield with Billy's dad and then oversaw Billy's first run on the football field as a six-year-old boy at Innisfail, went to see Billy train with the Devils. 'He looked all right, still at that stage you wouldn't have predicted to where he has got to now. You know the thing that struck me most about Billy was that there was a good man in there. That's where Billy shines through. He's a good man. The doors opened, but he was the one that made them open.'

Tommy Slater also saw Billy training with the Devils Colts and saw he had suddenly obtained the pace he'd been after all his career. 'He wasn't a kid anymore, he measured up and he'd developed a lot of speed. That was the thing that amazed me—how he'd changed, how he'd found all this speed.'

Billy stayed on because he had the track work gig with Myles Plumb, while Tommy's son James returned to Innisfail to find work. Many said James, who played in the centres, had as much potential as Billy at that stage of their careers. James kept playing at a regional level and later, after a stint in Innisfail, played for the Burleigh Bears. He had terrible knee injuries and one knee reconstruction forced him out of the game for two years. He later played for a regional Newcastle side. He stayed in touch with Billy and they often 'got on the punt' when Billy had some time off—a Slater tradition. 'He's a good kid,' said James, who is now a landscaper in Sydney.

Billy was soon a regular in the Colts side and was almost unstoppable, scoring in most games.

When he first played with the Colts he trialled on the wing. His experience had been as a halfback or at five-eighth. At one stage he even thought he'd be a great dummy half player but he was running into one of the best in the land in the burgeoning talent of Cameron Smith. So Billy played most of his whole Colts first season in the centres.

He developed an uncanny sixth sense with Cooper Cronk, working off Cronk's passing and kicking game. Cronk was an interesting player, intensely private and highly motivated. He'd grown up in rugby union and once played for the Australian schoolboys but then had crossed over to league.

Cronk once explained how he'd set himself almost impossible tasks as a young kid to improve his game. He grew up in Brisbane's southern suburbs and attended St

Laurence's College where rugby union was favoured. After school, he used to buy himself a packet of hot chips and go to the football field and tell himself he couldn't head home until he'd kicked ten goals in a row over the football posts from five different positions. Sometimes he'd be there in the dark until he achieved his task.

As Cronk was finishing school at St Laurence's one of his rugby coaches Gavin Darwin mentioned the talented Cronk to Storm football manager Mick Moore, who was a friend. Darwin said:

> It was in the late-90s that I was approached by Mick Moore and asked if I knew of any good young players, and that was around the time Cooper was finishing [school]. He had that league background at Souths Acacia Ridge and I asked if he would mind me mentioning his name to a few mates, so that's when I rang Hook [Andy Griffin]. They weren't overly thrilled with him at first and said 'Are you sure about this bloke?' It took him a little while to break through at [feeder club] Norths before he made it to the Storm and the rest is history.

Cronk had learned accuracy and dedication in his earlier days. And he was a good listener. His accuracy with his kicking and passing game was helping elevate Billy to his new heights at the Colts. Cronk, though, was playing in a utility role with the Colts and hadn't yet cemented the halfback position that he would make his own for Queensland and Australia.

Billy scored 34 tries in his Colts year, and he reckoned nearly thirty 'came off a Cooper Cronk pass'.

In one game, the Colts were smashing Souths Logan about 70–0. Almost everyone in the Norths side had scored a try except Billy.

'There was about ten minutes to go and Trent McKeough made a line break, was 20 metres from the line and could've scored himself but decided to lob over to me on the left and give me a try,' Billy recalled. 'The winger was coming across and I put the ball down and landed on my shoulder and did my AC joint. I was out for four weeks, but I got the try! '

Smith, Cronk and Billy were elevated into the Queensland Cup team for the Devils to play Ipswich in one senior game. Watching was teammate and halfback Kevin Carmichael, a senior player at the end of a long career that included stints at the old South Queensland Crushers and a cameo appearance with the Melbourne Storm. Carmichael was a loyal Norths player who started with them in 1993. The former Dalby boy was almost soldered onto the club and was a four-time winner of the Norths Player of the Year award.

He was amazed at how the young Billy accepted his elevation to the senior team with such confidence. Billy even started urging the players to move to the best field positions.

'He still made quite a few errors, which was normal for someone his age; he just had lightning speed. He was so electric, so willing to try things and so keen to play.'

Billy later lamented that coaches were trying to pull his head in when he experimented with his plays. 'We didn't have the pressure on us that young fellows have now in the under-20s. It was a good time in my life. I was never afraid to try stuff and coaches were always trying to pull me back from trying stuff,' Billy told Steve Ricketts.

On this day at Ipswich, the experienced Carmichael stood back in awe at the rookie seventeen-year-old. 'One thing that stood out, as a player back then, just the talk from a young fella at that stage of his career, how confident he was telling players what to do. I was so surprised to see a kid do that; and his speed was just amazing.'

'Cooper was a good talker too.' Carmichael developed a friendship with the young Cronk. Cronk was his apprentice plumber for almost two years. He became like a family friend as Carmichael dropped his kids off at various places for childcare or school in Brisbane in the morning before the master and his apprentice headed off to jobs. Cronk was learning his trade to be a plumber, not a footballer. At that stage being a professional football player was a pipe dream. Cronk would always call in at Christmas to see how the Carmichaels were going after that pipe dream was in full flow.

'Cooper is a little bit reserved. He's careful what he says to people, he just keeps things inside.' But out on the field, Cronk was a vocal motivator. 'At Devils team meetings both Cooper and Billy would always say what they thought. With a lot of young fellows they often just sit there with their arms folded and you have to drag things out of them, but not with those two.'

Carmichael went on to coaching positions at the Devils, firstly the reserve grade in 2002 and then the Colts in 2003. He'd sometimes travel down to the Storm headquarters in

Melbourne to help with pre-season training.

Billy had landed in the fold. He was surrounded by people who liked and respected him. In his second year in Brisbane he moved in with one of Carmichael's mates Wade Fenton, who was playing with Norths' senior team after a short stint at the Storm where he had five first class appearances. The boys set up lodgings at Wavell Heights, not far from Norths' headquarters.

It was a typical football players' share house with parties and lots of laughs and the smell of Dencorub. For Billy, though, he had to keep his social life in order because he was often up early to ride track work for Myles Plumb.

Billy still kept in touch with his Innisfail mate Paddy Gardner. One day they went to watch a Broncos game to see how the big-time players strutted their stuff.

'That will be us soon, eh Paddy,' an enthusiastic Billy told him.

Paddy lamented later: 'That was what happened for him, but not for me.' Paddy, though, had his own taste of glory, winning the prestigious Queensland Cup for his club Redcliffe in 2006.

Bandiera lived near Norths' home oval in Nundah and went to see how the young Innisfail recruit was going. 'I couldn't believe it, I'd been footballing and talent scouting for a while and I thought "this kid's got everything"—his footwork, his speed and his ball handling—he really stood out. I thought "they [Norths] are on a winner here."'

Billy's team were 2001 minor premiers but lost to Redcliffe in the grand final 24–22. Chris Fullarton was the Colt's coach. Fullarton liked country players because he believed they carried a degree of toughness that young city-raised players lacked. He was also on the lookout for good attitudes in the younger ranks. Suddenly in his coaching ambit, he had multiple players who were the cream of a generation.

What impressed him initially about Billy was his determination and strength of character. He'd found lodgings and work within a very short time of arriving in Brisbane. He wasn't asking for handouts or for more money; he was just getting on with his life ambition.

And Fullarton could clearly see his strong commitment at training—Billy was often the first one there and the last to leave. He was constantly trying to improve himself and at that stage of his career, he needed to. In his first year at Colts, his error rate was high, and he was still slight, not weighing much more than 80 kg.

Fullarton said:

> When I saw Billy had a job I thought, 'Things are going to work out well for that kid.' He was very independent. I played him a lot in the centres. He was a very brave player and sometimes his plays came off and sometimes they didn't. He was always cheerful and got on with the other players very well. He was only small but had this amazing pace. Both John Ribot and I saw him early on and we were impressed. He was a real try scorer.

Fullarton, who went on to coach the junior Australian league team, had a few ideas on how players should be able to handle themselves in attack and defence. He wanted them to be able to score a try one against one and to defend one on one. That was his benchmark for a player.

He also wasn't scared to blood Colts in the senior competitions. Billy was once pushed up to reserve grade and repaid the faith by scoring 4 tries in a game.

'John Ribot [the Storm boss] saw that and said "Who's that?" I said "Billy Slater". He turned and said "We'd better sign him up."'

Queensland league legend and Melbourne Storm franchise owner John Ribot was always a keen follower of Billy's career. He was as seasoned as anyone in the business side of sport. He'd handled all the punches as the CEO of Super League when Rupert Murdoch stepped fearlessly into the hornet's nest of tradition and signed up clubs for his new league venture. Ribot was already a Brisbane Bronco at heart, its first CEO, and then became the figurehead of the Super League push, putting his reputation and future on the line to secure Murdoch's aims, partly based on supporting Murdoch's pay TV arm, Fox. After a peace deal was struck between Super League and the ARL in 1997, the National Rugby League was formed. Ribot then boldly took on the Melbourne Storm franchise in the Aussie Rules–mad city. He had to kick down doors everywhere to find sponsors and get the Melbourne press behind the Storm. This was in a city where newspapers consistently ran fourteen pages of sports news just on Aussie Rules. He wasn't scared of a challenge.

Ribot was always angry at how the Sydney-centric ARL had ignored Queensland and its rich history of football, and sucked the talent from Queensland decade after decade. The State of Origin series had helped rectify that imbalance. He was sacked from an ARL sub-committee for daring to suggest that the league grand final be staged in Brisbane. As CEO of the new Brisbane Broncos he'd made a statement about the depth of talent in Queensland. The Broncos had been a huge success, and the State of Origin had pushed those ardent feelings of Queenslanders to the fore. By linking up with Norths Devils as the feeder club to the Storm, he was assuring his new club, the Storm, of a massive future. If it was meant to be or not, he'd set up a huge pipeline of talent flying from Queensland straight over Sydney and pumping straight into the Storm's reserves in Melbourne. In chess you might have called it a checkmate move. It would leave an indelible mark on the Storm and on rugby league.

Norths was also a powerful club. Anyone who worked there probably had at least played for Queensland, and many, including coach Andy Griffin, would reach greater heights in the game coaching the Broncos. Norths was like—if it could be compared to the horse racing industry—a place where the top trainers came to view the best young colts.

Billy arrived at the feeder club at a time when the mother-club, the Storm, was at a make-or-break point with sponsorship. They were struggling to meet deals to attract the big players, and being fined for going slightly over the salary cap. Their big hope was to get players from the grassroots up, young players that would stick loyally with the club.

When they found a player, they often looked at character first, and football skills later. If there was any chance their players might run off the rails, they didn't want to know about them. One of the most remarkable football births in league history was underway.

Ribot was an Origin and Australian league hero. He saw the young Billy go through his paces and was impressed, but not convinced he would make it in the big league.

Ribot had actually played against Billy's dad in his early league days and remembered Ronnie 'Mophead' Slater as a 'cheeky bugger'.

He was trying to re-fashion his idea of the Slaters when he saw Billy play for the first time. 'He was a skinny little guy but had incredible leg movement. At first sight you could tell his technique wasn't right, but then he worked so hard at his game, he's a great example of someone who gets there due to enormous determination.'

Young Norths Colts received just $5000 a season. Billy had hung in there and his contract was up to $22,000 a year, which included a clause to allow him to attend a three-month pre-season training camp at the Storm. Murray did the contract negotiations with Billy over the phone. In 2002, the rival NRL club Broncos showed a concerted interest in the young Innisfail dynamo, who was now playing the occasional game in the Queensland Cup.

Ribot was with Mark Murray at Nundah's Albert Bishop Park late in the season to watch a Devils game when they got a shock to see Broncos and Origin coach Wayne Bennett in the crowd at the small ground.

Murray remembers: 'I thought I'd call in and see who's doing what. Billy was on fire. Every time Billy got the ball he'd break the line.'

Ribot turned to Murray: 'Hey look over there, there's Benny [Wayne Bennett], what's he doing at a Colts game?'

Ribot knew Bennett was looking for some new strength players and, as expected, was assessing the Colts' talent pool. They suspected he was after Billy following his big debut season.

The suspicions were on the mark. Soon enough an offer came through from the Broncos wanting Billy to join them. They probably thought an out-and-out Queenslander like Billy, who loved the sunshine and surfing, would jump at a chance to join a Brisbane club for his senior career.

By this time the rising star Billy had engaged a manager, Geoff Bagnall, a former league player from the Gold Coast. Everyone knew Bagnall as just 'Bags'. He'd been recommended to Billy by Billy's godfather, Terry Koorockin, an old league buddy of Ronnie's who'd played at Valleys and Norths.

Koorockin told Bags: 'I've got a good footballer for you—my godson—he's pretty fast.' Bags went and saw Billy play at Norths and saw Billy run in 4 tries that afternoon. He knew straight away he was looking at someone special.

Bagnall was well known in Queensland league circles and was a Gold Coast Tweed Giants halfback from 1988 to 1991, with fifty-five first-grade appearances. He went overseas to play in Britain with Wakefield Trinity and returned to Australia in 1994 to become a Canberra Raider playing at halfback under Tim Sheens, the whole time in reserve grade. He was surrounded at the club by greats such as Ricky Stuart. He returned to the Gold Coast in 1995 to captain–coach and started managing younger players, slowly building up a portfolio of player clients. He juggled this work with his main living as a teacher.

It was a young seventeen-year-old Billy that came looking to him to up the ante in his career and Bags was more than delighted to help. The casual friendly atmosphere of the arrangement suited Billy.

When Billy first showed up at Bags's Gold Coast home, he couldn't believe his eyes. He'd rarely seen such a lovely home. Bag's wife Marissa commented later how Billy was 'such a well-mannered boy' and a 'lovely country kid'. Billy sat down to talk to Bags about his new contract hopes, still agog at the well-appointed unit.

'Love the pad you've got here Bags,' he said.

Bags replied: 'Don't worry Billy, you'll have four or five of these by the time you're finished playing.'

Bags wasn't far off the mark. As Bags set about negotiating Billy's new Norths–Storm contract, he took a call from Peter Nolan, the then Broncos recruitment officer, urging him to bring Billy to a meeting with himself and Bennett at the Broncos headquarters.

Bags and Billy turned up and were feted like kings as the youngster was shown around all the facilities, including the dressing room, to give him a taste of what it would be like to be a Broncos player.

Melbourne's offer, though, was better and was already on

the table. Ribot did everything in his power to get Billy down to Melbourne to trial for the Storm.

'We made the decision not to go with the Broncos by the time we were leaving their gates,' Bags remembers. 'He almost did become a Bronco but we felt he had more opportunities staying with Norths and having the incentives to go with the Storm. Anyway, Melbourne were offering more [money].'

Bagnall doesn't believe that any contract provision that would have required Billy to work at the Broncos Leagues Club had anything to do with Billy's decision. Although he was a dead-set hard worker and could look after himself, Billy thought if he got a proper football contract, he shouldn't have to work in another job.

Billy told his uncle Tommy 'I don't want to work and play, I just want to play footy.' Billy's dream of earning his way through life via football was about to come true. He was sticking firm to his ambitions.

The Broncos interest had forced the Storm to stoke up the ante to keep Billy in their fold. Billy was also blooded in his second year at Norths in the Queensland Cup teams where he was up against bruising encounters with players from Wynnum and the Burleigh Bears.

Fullarton said: 'He was only an eighteen-year-old lad and we put him in against some tough seasoned competitors in their late twenties and he got touched up a fair bit in the games. He was finding it hard in that division, and it was hard.'

Murray supported this blooding of the young players to see what they were made of.

Fullarton said: 'You could see it was very testing for them. Mark was a very tough disciplined coach and a lot of those good Storm players, including Dallas Johnson, came through that era. Dallas was one of my favourite players—he's a very courageous player.'

Johnson was Billy's old Far North adversary when Billy was again punching above his weight in the under-18s when his Innisfail side played Atherton in the grand final. The Herberton born Johnson was as tough as teak. Raised on a cattle farm, he was a laconic, hardy soul. He would become one of the fiercest tacklers the game had seen. Storm coach Craig Bellamy once lauded him as 'one of the finest one-on-one defenders of the modern era'.

Johnson reckons he ran over Billy 'twenty times' in their under-18s battle. 'We ended up winning that game pretty well. Who would have thought we'd end up in the same team for much of our careers?'

Johnson was a bit older than Billy and had made the trek to Norths the year before. 'He arrived in his shit-box Magna. They gave him a few trials and kept him on. He was just a natural player.' Both Johnson and Billy went down for pre-season training at the Storm in Melbourne.

The Far North was again stoking the fire of league's ranks.

Billy had a pre-season with the Storm in Melbourne—a training camp where they had intense skills training. Out-of-form Storm players or those returning from injury lay-offs often returned to the Norths fold to play and became mentors to the younger ones. One of those was Kirk Reynoldson. A big strapping forward (103 kg and 188 cm tall) with a big bushy bushranger-style beard, he would be pounding the sidelines with Billy (at 80 kg and 178 cm) running around markers on the ground. The pair would be training for an hour before the game.

'Kirk had a short mentor role with Billy, which was great,' said Fullarton.

The Storm also had housing for the young Colts on Storm contracts. Greg Inglis was one of those in the club's residential program. GI, as he was known, would also become one of the Storm's greats, coming into the fold just a bit after Billy.

If there was a renaissance in rugby league, it was all emerging out of the flourishing ranks of Norths.

Fullarton mixed it up sometimes with Billy once playing at halfback against Wests. As Billy was being tried out in different positions, he was gaining valuable experience about how the league team played.

'He was very keen to learn things, very keen to try things, he's a good student of the game,' Fullarton said.

Meanwhile, Fullarton said it took a while for Cronk to change from his rugby mindset to league. 'Cooper was always a very good defender and a very good kicker of the ball. Once again he had a good attitude and was a great trainer. At first, I thought he might just play first-grade and would be a good bench player and I thought he might be a dummy half.'

Of course, the arrival of Cameron Smith made sure no-one else was going to be dummy half in a Norths side he was in (although before he arrived at Norths, Smith had been playing halfback for Logan Brothers).

Smith was a talent right from the start. 'He was a standout, he didn't need much coaching.' Fullarton was amazed how Smith created time and space for his runners, constantly looking for faults in the defence line. He was a tireless performer on the field. 'When Cameron's going well, you don't see him. He's just giving everyone else good service of the ball. And when the other players drop off, or tire, he steps up to the plate.'

Fullarton happened to be in the right place at the right time with so many young talented players. The trio he helped train would be a force in rugby league for more than a decade.

Ribot walked up to Murray after Billy had gone down to the Storm and said: 'Can you get a few more of those Innisfail players for me?'

Murray told Bandiera later: 'I had all these young blokes when they came to the Colts complaining that they didn't have a job, didn't have a car and wanted more money, but what really stood out for me was that Billy did not once complain or ask for anything.'

While Smith and Billy Slater, who started at Norths in the same year that Cronk did, would earn contracts with Melbourne, Cronk took his time to progress. In 2003 he trialled with the Storm but did not impress the selectors and he had to return to Norths. He said:

> I had a terrible pre-season. Bill and Dallas [Johnson] stayed behind. I was sent back to Brisbane Norths. I dare

say Craig [Bellamy] had written me off, and a lot of other people had, too. To an extent, I probably did as well. I went back and enjoyed the good times that my mates were having, because they were working. I saw that as a little bit more important at that point in time, dropped the bottom lip for a while.

Billy, though, was on his way to a whole new world and it would take a couple of years before Cronk would rejoin Billy and Smith in the ranks of the surging Storm.

CHAPTER FOUR

MELBOURNE

Billy's journey to the southern climes of Storm's headquarters brought him both fame and the unlikely spin-off of anonymity. As Billy's career hit the radar, his rise rarely raised a bleep on the Aussie Rules mad–minds of Melbournians. Even after he achieved fame, he could walk down Collins Street without having his hand shaken or fielding a side glance. Back in his home state in the Queen Street Mall in Brisbane he'd be mobbed by fans.

The anonymity factor took away the pressure for Storm players. It was no surprise to see the Storm training in the centre of Melbourne at Gosch's Paddock, with no-one stopping to watch or traffic slowing to get a glimpse of the NRL stars, some of them Australian Test players. It was a surreal atmosphere for players feted in the other states.

Settling into a new city, not knowing anyone or the local culture, created a scenario where the young Storm players from Queensland bonded even more closely. They ended up living near each other or sharing houses, mainly in the inner-Melbourne suburb of Richmond, socialising together and talking the same talk on the football field.

It was a bond between Cronk, Smith and Billy that could never be broken. A bond that stood firm when big deals were put under their noses to move north and when all seemed lost after the salary cap crisis. Billy would stick with the club that had given him his start. He always felt part of the Storm family.

Billy, though, was not pleased when he arrived in Melbourne for the pre-season. He went there on the assurance that Mark Murray, one of his mentors from Norths Devils, would be the coach and that he would be getting some trial games after the pre-season training period. But there had been a major split in the ranks just before Billy arrived.

Ribot had called on Murray as an interim coach after the sudden departure of Chris Anderson after just seven rounds of the 2001 competition. Anderson, the Storm's foundation coach, was upset by the treatment of the Storm half Brett Kimmorley and Anderson's own son Ben, both of whom hadn't been re-signed by the Storm. Anderson claimed he was 'led down the garden path' by Storm hierarchy during the contract negotiations for the players. Anderson quit, but was quickly picked up by the Cronulla Sharks (who picked up Kimmorley as well). It was a bitter split.

Murray stepped into the breach. Ribot's mate was a disciplined coach and not afraid to make big decisions. Murray was part of a sea-change occurring at the Storm, where many of the old guard would leave and the new young colts move in. Instead of being a cobbled-together team, the Storm were refashioning their future from the ground up, putting faith in youth rather than tried stars, and recreating a club culture.

They had already done amazing things. In 1999 they secured their first premiership after just two years in the NRL. Nevertheless, things appeared to be falling apart at a senior level. The club was constantly making a loss and breaching the salary cap by small margins, incurring small fines. Clubs, just like Souths in their glory days or Manly in 2011, sometimes imploded or found it hard to capitalise on their success.

Murray said they were frustrating years as the Storm re-invented itself. As he tried to make some tactical changes, it eventually led to a player revolt when Murray sacked hardworking prop Robbie Kearns as captain midway through 2002. Kearns complained to the Storm leadership that he had been betrayed.

Murray had a gut feeling that some in his player group were out of touch and hadn't experienced the highs and lows of life, going straight from high school to be professional footballers without 'life experience'. He found it increasingly difficult to manage them.

'I made a decision to make some changes and that didn't go down well at the time. I thought the changes were in the best interests of the team. I thought we needed to change things to get the team moving,' Murray said.

The crisis point came with the Storm's poor 2002 year, finishing in tenth place—its lowest position in its short history. The players' leadership group, including Scott Hill, asked management to urge Murray to step down as coach. Ribot had to make the hard decision of removing his old mate—his Kangaroo buddy. If he stuck with Murray he risked division in the ranks and poor morale. At the brink, Ribot decided he'd urge his old mate to go.

Murray saw his axing as part of what happened in sport, part of the cut and thrust of life in the big league. 'I accepted the decision,' he said. He thought he was only there on an interim basis. Ribot paid out his contract.

Hill said it was a difficult time to raise the player concerns about Murray, but he felt something needed to be done.

> I just spoke the truth. It was very hard when players were just not comfortable with the coach. We had to voice our opinion at some point. I was the one who took it up and more or less I became the scapegoat. I think it was a good decision to speak my mind. I suppose down the line Craig [Bellamy] might never have been signed if we hadn't raised our concerns about Murray. But I still have a good relationship with Muppet [Murray].

The whole furore had the unlikely result of opening the door to a rookie coach who would become a mainstay of the club.

Enter the Dragon or, more specifically, the Raider. If players thought life was a little tough under Murray they didn't know what would be in store for them with the arrival of a coach whose nickname was 'Bellyache' (because he always seemed irritated).

The former top Canberra fullback, winger and centre was a vital part of the Raiders teams that won the 1989 and 1990 premierships. Bellamy was the understudy to master coach Wayne Bennett at the Brisbane Broncos when he was approached by Ribot to take on the helm at the Storm. His efforts as a consummate physical trainer and his no-nonsense approach had already been noted by those who knew the qualities needed to be a leader of an NRL team.

Born in the tough coal mining and power-producing town of Portland in the central tablelands of New South Wales, Bellamy was not afraid to blow his stack when he felt he needed to. He liked to play his music loud—Status Quo and The Angels— and he yelled his instructions loud. His belief was to always push players to a higher degree, mentally and physically. He was an exacting coach, expecting the highest standards on and off the field. It was sometimes a baptism of fire when the young bloods of the Storm arrived in Melbourne. For the experienced players it was good to have someone going to as much physical extremes as they were being asked to perform.

Players tell of him winning the first run with him as trainer; a punishing run on the strip known as The Tan along the Yarra River. Bellyache won the run by a space. He was also in the gym sweating away and grimacing alongside the players on the exercise machines and weights.

Kevin Carmichael helped with a lot of the pre-season training and said the new players found Bellamy 'scary'.

'He seemed pretty scary to all those younger boys when they first went down there. Billy would be helping him [Bellamy] in all his drills.'

Dean Lance was part of the Bellamy training package. Originally the former Raiders teammates had been in talks to coach at Wests Tigers, but they didn't want that deal, preferring to go with the Storm and persuaded by Ribot, whom they both liked.

Lance was an experienced player and coach—a former captain of the Raiders in their golden era with Meninga and Stuart. He went on to coach fleeting Super League teams in Perth and Adelaide before coaching Leeds Rhinos in Britain for three years.

Lance had contacts all over the place. He was the last captain of the Newtown Jets before they were cut from the major Sydney league competition. He formed lifelong friendships with people such as staunch Jets supporter and boxing trainer Johnny Lewis, whom he would sometimes get down to Melbourne to help motivate the Storm players.

Bellamy and Lance had always been close and their wives and families were great friends.

When their training partnership deal was accepted by Ribot they set up a unit in South Yarra together, cooking joint tucker and keeping their heads in computers as they remade the Storm. Lance would go back to his family on the Gold Coast when he could—sometimes they were apart for three months—and Bellamy would go back to his family in Brisbane when he could.

Lance and Bellamy had actually been league opponents for a while in 1981 when they played in the Newcastle competition: Lance from the West Newcastle Rosellas and Bellamy from the Macquarie Scorpions. They both had a country-boy-made-good feel about them—Lance was from Narrabri in north-west New South Wales. They knew a lot about toughness, but also how to have a good time. Lance always knew there was a huge part of super coach Wayne Bennett emerging out of the talent of Bennett's understudy Bellamy. (Bennett had coached them both at the Raiders in his brief stint there in 1987.) Lance became Bellamy's sideline man, shouting on-field instructions sent down from the coach's box.

Lance had already heard about Billy from his Gold Coast friend Terry Koorockin (Billy's godfather). 'He's quick, but he's small,' Koorockin told Lance. When Lance and Bellamy first saw Billy they weren't sure such a small kid would make it in the big time.

After an average season in and out of the Colts side, Billy was offered the chance to trial with the Melbourne Storm late in 2002. When he headed further south, he fully expected to be on a return plane to Brisbane. He trialled with his old North Queensland adversary Dallas Johnson. Two boys from the Far North were making the big time in the far south.

'As was always the case, Billy was leading the way in the training,' said Johnson. 'We ended up getting picked and making our debut together.'

Bellamy suddenly had at his disposal an array of rising young stars.

Billy had settled in well. He shared a flat with Johnson when he first arrived in Melbourne.

'We were all close from the start, all living around Richmond, going out at night together. Sometimes Matt

Geyer would pick us all up and take us to training,' said Johnson.

The Queensland players formed a little sub-clique in the Storm player web. It wasn't cliquey enough to create divisions in the team but everyone knew where they belonged.

After negotiations between Bagnall and the club, the Storm had Billy on a $40,000 a year contract with inbuilt incentives that included a $2000 bonus for each first-grade game appearance and a $150 a week rental subsidy. (Billy would play twenty-six times in 2003, meaning he earned an extra $52,000 on top of his contract money.) It was a good deal for a first-year player but Billy had to reach all the incentive benchmarks to make it worthwhile and make his time in Melbourne viable. Bagnall said Billy achieved all the benchmarks in the contract—an amazing feat.

New Storm coach Craig Bellamy saw potential in Billy where others didn't. And Billy's gamble had paid off, he'd broken through into professional league and now he just needed to persevere and wait for a bit of luck to make his first-grade debut.

Bellamy explained why Billy had impressed him:

> It was his speed and elusiveness and his willingness to be wherever the footy was.
>
> It was funny, because I'd spoken to a few people about him before he came down here and they didn't have a big rap on him. They thought he was a bit frail and a bit off defensively. It was true, he didn't have a great tackling technique, but he wanted to learn.

> He was willing to put his body on the line and he took every chance that came his way to show what he could do at training. He was a good listener, a quick learner and desperate to know what first-grade footy was all about.

It was still hard yards for young Billy, but circumstances would open the door. At the start of the 2003 season, many of the Storm players carried injuries. The body of the man he would finally replace was falling apart all around him from the tough rigors of first-grade football.

Billy was concerned though, he was about to start his career—Murray had left and he had no idea what Bellamy was like. 'I was dirty that Mark Murray wasn't coach any more because when I signed, Mark said he would give me two trial games after the pre-season and I didn't know who this Craig Bellamy bloke was,' Billy said.

'There were about eight fighting for two spots,' said Billy. 'I just knuckled down and gave it a really good shot and at the end of the pre-season Craig wanted to keep me and Dallas Johnson here. We played a couple of trial games and I ended up as fullback for Melbourne Storm in round 1 2003 against Cronulla. I was just so proud to have got through such hard work.'

Billy had impressed in the trial games. He scored 4 tries against a Victorian representative team and then impressed against an experienced Rabbitohs outfit.

'Back then he [Bellamy] was very intimidating, didn't smile very much and wasn't very happy most of the time.

As a young fella you didn't want to go near him. As we've got older we have a great relationship with Craig,' Billy said. 'I thought he was a cranky bugger, but it was just his uncompromising fashion. Work ethic always comes first for Craig. He despises those who take short-cuts, so I made it my mission to impress.'

Dean Lance said Bellamy learnt as much as he could from his time working alongside Bennett at the Broncos. The perfectionist of Bennett emerged in the training manual of Bellamy and it meant he would not let problems slide. He'd pull up the play at training and fix a problem on the spot—he'd never let things fester or tick over to a later date.

Although Johnson and Billy quickly adapted to life in Melbourne, they were in shock at what their new master Bellamy had in store for them at training.

Bellamy designed a punishing training schedule. Studley Park is described as one of Melbourne's most relaxing havens with a boathouse on the bend of the Yarra—but it was no haven for the Storm boys. From Christmas he had the team doing 7 km or 8 km hill runs (on a hill the boys soon hated) in Studley Park. Not just once a week, nor twice: they were required to do three hill runs a week without fail. Bellamy was even known to leap out from behind a tree if he found a player not putting in on the run. 'Studley Park is a beautiful place but I got to hate the sight of it,' remembers Johnson.

They also put in hard training at Ruffey Lake Park, known to everyone as Ruffeys. Bellamy had his team fit for the start of the 2003 season.

The Storm had a system of older players mentoring the new arrivals. Five-eighth Scott Hill did a lot of the early work with Billy and was his weights partner. He was a great friend to have and was part of the leadership group—a group Billy would later join. The leadership group not only went to management with their concerns but they also approached players if they thought they were getting out of line.

Hill was foundation player at the club but had suffered a terrible knee injury just before the Storm won the premiership in 1999. Hill was forced to watch from the stands after undergoing a knee reconstruction. Missing out on a grand final win always disappointed him. (He would get another chance in 2006, but the Storm would lose to Brisbane, despite Hill's magnificent effort in setting up 2 tries.)

Hill knew how luck could help play a part in a career. He was right on the spot when Canterbury were looking for someone to replace the legendary Terry Lamb when Hill made his league first-grade debut in 1996. The doors would open for Billy in a similar way at the Storm.

Hill was part of the move to the Storm by almost the entire backline of the Hunter Mariners after the death of Super League to the newly born NRL competition. The slippery five-eighth from Forster in New South Wales had powered into the NSW Origin and Australian sides in 2000.

When Hill first saw Billy he knew Billy 'was definitely something in the making'. Billy was with the players in a touch footy training squad in the pre-season and Hill said Billy hit the ground running, already directing plays among the senior team.

'What I do remember when he first came down was that he had long hair well past his shoulders,' said Hill. Billy soon had a sharp clip for his debut game.

'During the whole pre-season he was always up the front in the runs and leading the way.'

In the weights sessions, Hill could see how Billy worked hard to increase his upper body strength.

While the young Billy was growing by the day, regular Storm fullback Robbie Ross was struggling with his fitness and battling a run of injuries as long as his arm. Ross took Billy under his wing and did an enormous amount of work showing him the intricacies of being a mobile fullback and how support play can ignite a team. Hill reckons Ross had an immense effect on young Billy's game. 'A lot of Billy's strength, in his ability to read a game and to give that support to the backline, came from Robbie Ross,' Hill said.

Ross was a Newcastle find. He played with the Newcastle Knights in 1994 and then moved to the Brisbane Broncos in 1996, playing alongside greats such as Alfie Langer and Darren Lockyer. He then played with the hastily concocted Hunter Mariners in 1997 during the short-lived Super League competition.

Ross was a young footballer on the New South Wales central coast and one of his best friends was Steve Monie, the son of legendary Parramatta and British Wigan coach John Monie. Monie, at that time training Parramatta, would make a special effort each week to come back and train up the Ourimbah under-13s when Ross was kicking off in the game. Once, Ross went with the Monies to a Parramatta game where Monie was coaching the likes of Peter Sterling, Eric Grothe and Ray Price. A young Ross sat in the players' area and couldn't believe his luck when he was greeted by his league heroes. (Ross was thrilled later in his career to play Monie's team Wigan.)

Ross had an important place at the Storm. He was the first player to be signed to play for the club. Ross said it happened over a few beers late one night at a pub with 'Reebs' (John Ribot) as the Hunter Mariners disappeared off the league map into history with the end of the Super League war. He and most of the Hunter Mariners backline were signed up for the Storm. 'I think I was just the first person to put pen to paper,' he said. News Limited's fingers were all over the move to get players from the defunct Hunter Mariners down to the Storm. But going to Melbourne suited Ross. His father had just moved there for a bank job with ANZ and he had his family close by.

Ross's best season was in 1999, when he scored a club-record 19 tries and then had a dominant State of Origin series for NSW, scoring the quickest try in Origin history. It was the first Origin try scored at Stadium Australia and the fastest—just forty-one seconds after kick-off. In the second game of Origin, Laurie Daley started the move, passing to Ryan Girdler who ran 40 metres before passing on to Ross who finished off the amazing sequence. Unfortunately, it was a drawn series and Queensland kept the trophy as titleholders.

After the series Ross earned an Australian jumper. A bloodied and jubilant Ross celebrated the Storm's maiden premiership that year.

'That was so exciting, but as happens with those moments I can't remember too much of that day,' he said.

But injuries plagued his career. A torn anterior cruciate ligament meant he only played thirteen games in 2000, then a hamstring injury disrupted his 2001 season where he played fourteen games. Groin and hamstring injuries meant he would play just eleven games in 2002. What was really lurking behind Ross's injury sheet was something much worse, a major problem in his vertebrae, a bulging disc that would eventually force him into early retirement from league and require six screws to fuse two vertebrae. When the doctor advised him he should retire to save his body he was actually relieved to end years of forlorn comebacks.

Ross's injury list was running out of control when Billy was about to start his career. A hip flexor injury added to his hamstring and groin injuries. Intriguingly, Ross places the whole list down to one knee injury in one tackle when the Storm played the Warriors. Doctors grafted ligament from his hamstring area for his crippled knee, then he had recurring hamstring injuries. He surmises this eventually led to some imbalance in his body and his back injury and bulging disc.

But he was eager to help Billy—for Billy's sake and also for the club, to which Ross had undying allegiance. He said it was always an honour to know that in the Storm locker room for the fullback position, Billy's name was there straight under his name. The 1999 premiership win had instilled a serious bond among players with their club struggling to get a foothold in Melbourne.

He remembers taking Billy and some of the other new players out at night to a restaurant that epitomised Melbourne—Pellegrini's—an Italian espresso bar in Bourke Street. They'd often go there for a pasta and coffee. (About ten years later Ross ran into Billy and asked him how he was going with the new players at Storm. 'Fine,' Billy said. 'I take them to Pellegrini's'.)

Ross ran through the essentials of being a fullback with Billy. Ross felt it was a generational show of faith after fullback Robbie O'Davis had done the same mentoring for Ross at the Newcastle Knights.

His help—as far as he could help such a talent—amounted to picking the right time to join in the backline and little hints such as catching the football on the full. He taught Billy how to get ready for the danger players and not to rely on just following the ball play—a trait Billy had when he first came to the Storm.

Ross also showed him how to read a kicker—a right-hand kicker would probably kick to the right of the field and vice versa for a left-hand kicker. He helped Billy determine the best field position to take as an opposition kicker moved in to the play. He also helped Billy perfect the numbers game—knowing how many players he should have on each side of the ruck and knowing where to send players either way as they came back to the defensive line after a tackle.

Dallas Johnson describes what became a constant in a Storm match playing with Billy: 'There I was, pulling my head out of some guy's arse, in a daze, and not knowing where to go and there's Billy sending me left or right to shore up the numbers.'

Ross did everything in his power to help the novice fullback and Billy would always remember him for what he did. Billy knew him by the nickname 'Boo Boo', a moniker Ross collected when he was sixteen when some old bloke on the sidelines reckoned he looked like the cartoon character Boo Boo the Bear. (Billy never earned an outrageous nickname like his mates, dad or grandad, he was always just 'Billy' or 'Slats'.)

Ross ran through videos and showed Billy the correct positional and support plays. He also got out his scrapbook to show Billy his successes.

Training him up was an honour, according to Ross. As Ross saw his career falling into shreds, Billy's star was rising.

At times, Ross hated the world for what was happening to him. He was at a mental peak, but his body was in injury free-fall. The frustration was tearing away at him. Ross said:

> I was pretty much on my last legs with injuries and I was just frustrated with the game too.
>
> When Billy arrived he was full of energy and full of cheek, in terms of his brilliance. At training no-one could catch him, he was like Speedy Gonzales.
>
> What was amazing was his speed on the ground and that it didn't change when he was carrying the ball. Normally you lose up to 10 per cent of your pace running with the ball than without it, but with Billy it hardly made any difference. Most players will tighten up somewhat.

> Billy had these big mitts and could carry the ball easily when he ran.
>
> You could tell from early on he was individually brilliant.

Ross had added another injury to the list as the first game of the season approached—a hip flexor injury. With Ross forced out, it was Billy's chance to shine. Bellamy showed huge faith in putting Billy straight into the line-up for the first game of the season.

Bellamy had gathered everyone together in the Storm's boardroom at the start of the season for a major talk. In an impressive speech, he told everyone how important it was to create a culture at the club. That was, to create respect and discipline. The players were stunned by the earnestness of Bellamy's speech. It stayed and echoed in their minds.

Billy was amongst friends. Cameron Smith had already played two games for the Storm in 2002, at halfback, but was now slotted in for hooker for 2003. This day was just his third first-grade game. Dallas Johnson was also making his debut. (Cooper Cronk was waiting in the wings at Norths Devils, still perfecting his kicking game before he would join the Storm in 2004.)

* * *

It was a bright sunny day after overnight rain and the day was warming up for autumn. Billy's dad Ronnie made the trip down from Eubenangee swamp, near Innisfail, to watch

Billy make his debut for the Storm at Toyota Park by Botany Bay in southern Sydney on 16 March 2003. Billy and his team walked out into a sea of Shark supporters' streamers and dancing Shark cheerleaders. He was hoping the Storm would resurrect their fortunes from the difficult 2002 season. It was like everyone was driving a new car and was eager to see how it went.

The whole day was a gamble on youth and inexperience. In the Sharks line-up were two youthful players, Paul Gallen and Greg Bird (set later to make their mark on Origin football for New South Wales and for Australia). David Peachey, the best fullback in the country, was holding the fort for the Sharks with his electric brilliance. The Storm's former half Brett Kimmorley was the Sharks captain and hoping to run amok amongst his old teammates. The Storm's foundation coach, Chris Anderson, still hurting from his falling out with his old club, was coaching the Sharks and eager to show his old team who was the boss.

The Melbourne side was heaped with rookies and experienced players alike. There was Scott Hill and Matt Orford, Robbie Kearns and David Kidwell, and captain Stephen Kearney. The rookies were Johnson, Smith and Billy. Smith looked like a fresh-faced pup, as did Cronulla's Bird, both of whom would become gritty combatants in later years in State of Origin. Leading the Storm was first-time coach Craig Bellamy, risking all with his brave selections.

If someone had a crystal ball to see into the future on that day, there couldn't be a more hyped set of circumstances in just a regular NRL game on a quiet warm Sunday afternoon. The

Sharks were coming off the back of a great 2002 season and expecting 2003 to be their season. Both teams were loaded with brilliance and potential. The atmosphere was electric.

Billy was supposed to be in the centres but in a late change his mate Matt Geyer moved to the wing and Billy was thrust into the fullback position. Billy ran on to the ground in a number four jumper—he'd been playing in the centres during the trials. Billy was noted as soon as he came on the field. 'Young Billy Slater looks dangerous every time he touches the ball,' commentator Warren Smith exclaimed. But what started as a pleasant autumn day was soon looking like an afternoon massacre for the Storm. Cronulla ran riot and had 18 points in even time on the board before the Storm even knew they were in Sydney.

The Cronulla cheerleaders were exhausted from celebrating. The commentators hailed Cronulla's start as a 'March carve-up'. 'They are in danger of being taken out of the game in the first half,' Fox Sports' Warren Smith exclaimed. Bird was one of the Cronulla scorers (just the third try of his first-grade career), but his elation was soured after he was placed on report for a head slam on the Storm's Rodney Howe.

In one of the early Cronulla tries, Billy latched on to the back of the Cronulla player as he went in to score. Billy was hanging on like he was cow-roping. 'A big man will always run over a little man,' Fox Sports co-commentator and former Raider and international Laurie Daley said. (Daley himself would end up seeing Billy as his side's nemesis when Daley later became the Blues coach.)

The Storm were down 22–0 and well on the back foot. The commentators started talking about Billy's size and his history as a track work rider. 'You don't see many jockeys or track work riders make it into the top grade football,' Smith said. 'I don't know of any,' Daley commented, adding that little Alfie Langer was the size of a jockey, but didn't know if he ever worked as a hoop.

Within moments of the comments, Billy was racing away and had suddenly swung the momentum of the match Melbourne's way with an explosive burst from dummy half. In one of his first touches in the game, he took the ball near the halfway mark and ran through the Sharks attack like a knife through butter, dodging one of the fastest players in the game, David Peachey, leaving him standing cold as if he'd just seen a ghost. Billy ran away towards the corner carrying the ball like it was a lightweight toy, weaving and jigging to score. A young Paul Gallen vainly tried to tackle Billy as he fell over the line with his momentum—a forerunner of Origin battles to come. It was the rugby league public's first taste of Billy the entertainer.

Warren Smith said: 'Slater scores like he was booting home a winner at Randwick. He notches up the first try of his career and what a way to do it on debut here.'

Bellamy was already telling people how impressed he was with Billy even before his first-grade debut.

Daley said: 'Speaking to Craig Bellamy over the last two weeks he's been telling me about Billy Slater and how he can find his way to the try line. He's got tremendous acceleration.'

Billy remembers the game:

We were down 22–0 after twenty minutes. It was daunting, but I was just out there loving my footy and enjoying playing first-grade in front of a big crowd.

We had a scrum 20 metres from our own line and I got into dummy half—that was the player I was then, I just wanted to be around the footy.

So I picked it up from dummy half, saw a gap and went down the short side. David Peachey came across and I stepped inside him and just pinned the ears back, put the head down and went for the corner and scored.

Ronnie was shouting and encouraging Billy from the sidelines.

The Storm came out firing in the second half and had clawed back almost the entire deficit, trailing 32–24 with just six minutes to play after 3 tries to Steve Bell and 1 to Matt Geyer. With five minutes remaining, Matt Orford ran from the scrum base to score under the posts untouched, taking the score to 32–30, after the conversion. Melbourne were miraculously in the game after being written off just minutes earlier. Greg Bird was running to the line with minutes to go when Billy picked him up and swung him to the ground like he was a bag of chaff. If there were any doubts about his defensive skills they were quickly fading in such a dominating display.

Close to the Storm line, Brett Kimmorley put in a poor grubber kick, which hit the foot of Storm second-rower Peter Robinson, who then picked up the loose ball, passed it on to Bell. Bell passed it over to Geyer who sped away to end a length of the field movement to stun the Sharks. Geyer punched the air and raised his fingers in amazement, as if he had just won a grand final.

There was controversy at the end. When the full-time siren sounded the referee refused to blow full-time, claiming the ball had gone off a Melbourne hand over the sideline after the Cronulla kick-off. Billy came rushing in to have his two cents worth as the referee ordered a scrum after full-time. Cronulla raced towards the line in the last play but were held back and the Storm were victors. The Cronulla cheerleaders were deflated—their pom poms at their sides—as the stunned Cronulla crowd filed forlornly out of Toyota Park.

Daley said it was one of the greatest comebacks he'd seen and showed 'the strength and character of the Storm'. 'Craig Bellamy will be ecstatic,' he said.

'That was Billy's debut and Craig Bellamy's debut as a coach,' Ronnie Slater remembers. 'Both of them never looked back. He had a great bond with Craig.'

Billy scored 2 tries in his next game in his first season against the Panthers and a month later he scored 2 tries in an electrifying display to again defeat the Sharks, this time at Olympic Park in Melbourne.

Olympic Park was the first ground of the Storm. It was nicknamed 'the Graveyard' because so many visiting teams lost there. It had such poor viewing facilities that visiting commentators from Sydney often complained they couldn't see the game properly. Storm had spent $5 million doing the old stadium up, but forgot to install new turnstiles, which sometimes led to large queues of people waiting to get into the ground.

Nevertheless, with players like Billy the turnstiles were about to get a real makeover and punishment. Bellamy reckoned he hadn't seen a player make such a sensational debut since Brad Fittler and Tim Brasher.

Ross made it back for one game in the interim but he would only make five appearances for the season, leaving the gate open for Billy to make his mark.

The Storm player group, though, was in tatters. Bellamy was struggling with a long injury list. In a disastrous situation, Bellamy had lost twelve players from his squad to injury. Hardy prop Rodney Howe was out for fifteen weeks with a knee injury, Jake Webster was out for the season and Steve Bell was also out with a knee injury. Scott Hill was carrying a shoulder injury. Centre Aaron Moule had a severe osteitis pubis problem that would force him within weeks to abandon his career at the Storm.

The Storm didn't have many places to turn to as they faced a tough Newcastle side in round 3. Although Bellamy at first said he wouldn't risk bringing back Ross, now he didn't have an alternative. Billy was put into the centres. 'It wasn't hard to pick because we've only got about seventeen blokes left,' Bellamy said. 'It's certainly not ideal but there's not much we can do about it.'

Bellamy said:

> I'm not prepared to risk blokes. But not just that; I know a 50 per cent or 70 per cent player isn't going to do as

good a job as a 100 per cent fit player, even if he's not as experienced or as talented.

We're not going to risk Robbie, and at the same time we're not going to put down the team's chances by playing someone on reputation if he can't go out there and do the job because of an injury.

Bellamy ended up playing him. He was putting a lot of pressure on his rookies including Billy. 'The more experience they get, the better they are going to be,' he said. 'It's certainly not ideal at the moment for us, but down the track we are going to get some benefit from having to play these young guys a little before their time.'

The Storm lost to Newcastle and the news was worse in late April when Moule announced he was hanging up his boots, throwing away hundreds of thousands of dollars in potential contract money at the time.

Moule told *The Age* he had 'had enough' of waking at 4 am with a sore groin,

> ... or not being able to sleep on my shoulders, waking up with dead arms. I'm sure many other footballers put up with this kind of injury and pain. Whether I've just hit my breaking point, I don't know. I just can't do it anymore. Thinking of how will I be when I'm thirty-five and forty—will I be able to bend over, will I able to get in and out of the car? I just had to evaluate to myself what that was worth.

He would later resurrect his career in England.

The next year, Billy would face the same injury crisis as Moule.

By the middle of the year Billy was a serious NRL proposition and had knocked back a long-term contract because he didn't believe it was enough. There was talk he might even move to the Roosters or Brisbane.

He had settled in well and was now enjoying Melbourne. He even did some cross-training with North Melbourne and Carlton. He loved surfing at Torquay and at Bell's Beach, sometimes with teammate Robbie Kearns.

Kearns was ecstatic to have Billy in the team.

'He's definitely been the brightest spark to come into the NRL in the past five or six years,' he said.

Kearns liked the audacity in Billy. 'Without being a bighead, he's got that little bit of arrogance about him,' he told Mark Fuller of *The Age*. 'But that's a good thing.'

Kearns said Billy would have to avoid the 'second-year syndrome'. 'One season doesn't make a player,' said Kearns.

As the season drew to a close, Blues coach Phil Gould declared Slater had been 'nothing short of a sensation'.

If Billy was injured he'd often just pack up his bags and head home to Innisfail. 'He knew there was always a bed here,' said his dad Ronnie. Billy was a bit scratchy in his first few press interviews. 'He's a pretty laid-back sort of a bloke, eh,' said Ronnie. 'He just loves his horses and footy.' Whenever Billy was asked who the greatest influence on his career was, he'd always say, without hesitation, 'my dad'.

Journalist Jackie Epstein conducted the first major press interview with Billy for the *Sunday Herald Sun*, in which he outlined his ambitions. Already he was being compared to some of the modern greats of the game in his first season. 'I got the opportunity to stay down here in the full-time squad, and then [coach] Craig [Bellamy] gave me the opportunity in first-grade with the injuries we had,' Slater told her.

'I'm off contract at the end of next year, but I like Melbourne and I'm happy to stay.'

The article compared Slater to 'a young Brad Fittler or Tim Brasher. His name had even been thrown up as a surprise candidate for Queensland State of Origin selection.'

Billy told Epstein: 'I hope what I've done can inspire young fellas to give it a go. I was never in Queensland sides when I was going to school. I just think if you really want something, you can put your head down and you'll get it.'

Billy had the Rookie of the Year award in the bag but a player dispute with the NRL led to the cancellation of the Dally M Awards. He'd always be disappointed he never got to hang that medal around his neck.

Billy was thrust into the pressure of finals football after Ross was told by doctors in August to sit out the season after he was diagnosed with a bulging disc in his back.

But while the injured brigade grew, the Storm managed to resurrect their fortunes and by the end of the season were in fifth place with a strong chance of making the grand final. They defeated the Canberra Raiders 30–18 at Canberra in the qualifying final.

Both Bellamy and Lance, former Raiders, took great heart out of beating their old team. (Bellamy also got the same thrill of beating his former coaching mates at the Broncos.) Lance said: 'We gave our players the reason to beat our old team and that energy flowed on to them.' The Raiders were relentlessly pummelled by the Storm from the time Bellamy took over. For eight years the Storm taught Canberra a football lesson and it wasn't until round 16 in 2009 that they were finally able to beat a Bellamy-led Storm. Since Bellamy has been at the Storm, they have only beaten the Storm four times in twelve years (up until July 2014).

Billy had cemented his place in the Storm as the highest try scorer of the year with 19 tries. Eventually the Storm were knocked out of the finals, blown away 30–0 in the semifinal by the Bulldogs (who had also thrashed Storm 50–4 in their previous encounter). But it had been nothing but a successful year for Billy and he had stamped his presence in the top league ranks.

Billy had arrived in Melbourne, starred in his first year and had come just a game away from getting through to a grand final and holding up the most coveted trophy in league. No-one knew at the time that Billy was suffering a potentially debilitating injury that would threaten his career.

CHAPTER FIVE

DAZZLER

Billy was hot property by the start of his second year in first grade. His early league connections faded as he soared into the higher stratosphere of sponsorship and six-figure contract deals. Senior players were urging him to get a new manager, telling him he needed greater firepower to extract his true worth.

It was a tough decision when he decided to split with his family friend 'Bags' Bagnall who had helped manage his affairs in the few years leading up to his Storm contract. Billy joined SFX Sports and took on a new manager, George Mimis, who had about ten years of knowledge in the business.

Sydney-based Mimis was a tough negotiator. An economics graduate from the University of Sydney, he'd set up his own sports management business and was able to work in all areas of sport from day-to-day issues, contract negotiations, media appearances and TV deals.

Billy decided he wanted someone with greater reach in the industry to take him forward. It came at a time when Bagnall, still a part-time manager, was negotiating a new contract for Billy with the Storm, with the new deal sitting on the table under the nose of Ribot.

Billy told his old friend the hard news: 'Bags, I'm going to get a full-time manager.'

'I just said "no worries"', Bagnall said.

Mimis had come in from the side without Bags knowing about it, but Bags didn't mind, he had his teaching career to pursue, though he still had part of his contract to run with Billy.

'I'm not upset about what happened or what didn't happen then. It's all positive and Billy has gone on to do great things. I know if I ever want him to come to my school for a sports day to see my students he'd be there in no time,' Bagnall said.

With his new contract, Billy hit pay dirt. Whatever he'd earned in his previous contract was the base amount for his next one. Just a year into the game, after negotiations, his new contract was upwards of $250,000 a year. Storm had made a big statement on what worth they placed on the best rookie in the competition.

No-one knew that later in the year Billy's career would be on the line with a serious groin injury. Bagnall said he had seen no sign of the injury when he saw Billy play in his first season. Doctors later surmised the injury was lurking for the last part of his first year and for all of 2004.

Billy's time had come. After battling injuries for years, foundation fullback Ross was forced out of the game with a bulging disc in his back, just as the 2004 season was about to get underway. The Storm decided to place part of its future on the young shoulders of Billy.

Ross announced his devastating news in March.

'The specialist has told me straight that I couldn't play the way my back is. If I was to have a fusion, it wouldn't make any difference. It was pretty final. I was told my future after footy would be at risk if I tried to play on,' Ross told the press. 'To be honest it is a bit of a relief that it is finally all over. I'm glad that I won't have to go through another rehab session; that I won't have to face the stress you go through each time you get injured.'

Ross was a victim of the new era of league, the hard punishing culture that demanded the best out of everyone, every time.

Coach Craig Bellamy offered Ross a job to work with the backline at the Storm as an assistant coach. 'Robbie is a popular guy among the players,' Bellamy declared. 'He is keen to have a role and I think he can bring something to the team.' He would still work closely with Billy and have that important mentoring role.

Finally, Cooper Cronk had joined the Storm's squad—he could hardly be ignored after scoring nearly 40 tries for Norths the previous year. He was the playmaker that would help ignite Billy's career. The three Queensland amigos were back together.

The Storm started 2004 poorly, losing three of their first four matches. They were wallowing in eleventh place, but because of a close competition, two wins suddenly had them up to fifth spot by round 7.

One of the new recruits was Ben MacDougall, the brother of Newcastle player Adam 'Mad Dog' MacDougall, one of league's true characters and a hero of the Newcastle Knights.

Unfortunately Ben MacDougall's year started badly with an injured hamstring and he missed a chance to play against his two brothers, Adam and Luke, in Storm's clash with the Rabbitohs in April. The Storm ran over the Rabbitohs 50–4.

MacDougall was discarded by Manly with two seasons left on a handshake contract agreement. He threatened to sue over it. He was from a phenomenal football family. All four MacDougall brothers—Adam, Luke, Ben and Sam—would all play top flight football.

MacDougall loved his new life at the Storm. He helped shore up a weak backline after the departure of Moule. He was in a confident mood and his first few games were great.

'I think I've probably been playing some of my best footy in the couple of weeks before I got injured,' he declared.

He'd thought of joining his brothers at Souths but his respect for Bellamy made him go with the Storm. Also, former Manly coach Peter Sharp, whom MacDougall knew, had just been made assistant coach at the Storm.

Adam gave him some advice he always heeded. 'I remember my brother saying to me only a couple of years ago that every player starts at the same point every pre-season, regardless of what they've done before,' MacDougall said.

MacDougall ended up sharing a house with Billy during the year.

Sharp, who coached Manly from 1999 to 2003 and left after board ructions in the Manly camp, joined the Storm as assistant coach with former Raiders captain Dean Lance alongside. Sharp was happy to have some clear air from the Manly in-fighting and enjoyed the new calm environment at the Storm. Both he and Lance were both doing the shuffle back to their families, Sharp back to Sydney, and Lance back to the Gold Coast. The home away from home atmosphere built up a big rapport between coaching staff and players. Bellamy's family were also still in Brisbane and he travelled home as often as he could.

Sharp was immediately impressed by the Storm set-up. Bellamy looked right at home after just a year at the helm. The club had overcome its more troubled times and was slowly rebuilding into a dangerous physical outfit.

Sharp hit the ground running during the big pre-season training as Bellamy worked everyone to maximum exhaustion. 'Craig was hard on them, tough on them,' Sharp says. 'It's a great footy club, outstanding, and we all bonded us three middle-aged "bachelors"—Craig, Dean and I!'

Sharp remembers when he saw Bellamy's first coaching performance when Storm were being thumped by Cronulla 22–0 in the first game of 2003, he said to himself 'this bloke won't last long'. Storm came back to win the game and Sharp then thought 'this bloke'll go a long way!' It was the first time he'd seen Billy too and thought he was 'just electric'.

Then a year later, he was coaching right beside them. He helped Bellamy put the players through a rigorous, physical pre-season for 2004, a regime most of the squad hated. Sharp worked mainly with the Storm backline.

Sharp said:

Billy was a great kid, very approachable, eager to learn, they were all kids then, Smith, Billy and Cronk.

You could tell how much they work on their game individually, that was also with great credit to Bellamy as well.

They'd work on all their little intricacies. They have some lovely set plays, work lovely lines. Billy worked hard on his timing and his carrying, they all worked hard on that.

The three formed the ultimate partnership. They were all nice respectful kids with a love of life and a love of footy.

Sharp didn't notice any problems among the squad, unlike many football teams. The Storm didn't have a drinking culture.

The Storm's secret weapon was often the fear-factor for teams visiting Olympic Park (a rundown old athletics field). Visiting teams couldn't handle the heat of the cauldron atmosphere with the Storm supporters, the purple army, right on the edge, breathing down their necks. The cold and rainy weather that often swept across Olympic Park was also an abrupt shock for many teams.

Sharp sometimes filled in as the main coach when Bellamy went away. Wayne Bennett personally asked the Australian Rugby League to have Bellamy with him on the Test coaching staff, even though there was no assistant coach position. It was a prelude to Bellamy joining the Test coaching team in an official position in 2005. Bennett and Bellamy respected each other. When Bennett indicated he was staying on at the Broncos in 2005, Bellamy immediately ruled himself out of any talk about moving there from the Storm with his contract up for renewal. Bellamy's manager John Fordham and Storm boss John Ribot sat down for new contract negotiations in the typical 'umming and ahhing' position. No-one was in any doubt Bellamy would put his lot in with the Storm again.

Sharp was a talented coach to have at the Club's disposal when Bellamy was away on Test duties. He oversaw the Storm's 28–6 demolition of the Cowboys in April, making it ten wins in a row for the Storm at Olympic Park. The stadium had a fortress-like effect on visiting players.

Sharp told *The Age*:

> It's an indication that it's a pretty reasonable footy side, that you can turn up and not be on the pace and a bit off the money and ground out a good victory. That aspect of it was terrific. We lacked a bit of shape and a bit of awareness around the footy all night. I don't know what that was, because last week we were quite good, the fact that we were good around our two halves and around our dummy half, but tonight we were just a bit out of shape.

Matt Geyer returned from a knee injury to score a first half-try in the game.

Meanwhile, Ross quit four months into his mentoring role. Injuries were agony, but what hurt more for a seasoned player was watching teammates excel on the field while he was out of play. He needed to turn to something else, a life revolution. It was a wise decision. His determination led to a successful career in finance. (He now oversees major property developments in London, using his great finance brain.)

There was a huge surprise waiting for Billy in the wings. Suddenly he was in calculations for Origin selection. Queensland selectors had decided to enlist some new blood, as the Maroons went through a transformation period after a remarkable era relying on stars such as Alfie Langer, Lote Tuqiri, Gorden Tallis and Wendell Sailor.

A young Cameron Smith and a young Slater were suddenly carrying Queensland's hopes after the Maroons lost the Origin 2003 series to New South Wales. Smith had played in the last Origin game of the series and his star was already on the rise, playing a hand in the final game drubbing of NSW. The victory had steeled Queensland for a winning 2004 Origin series.

The hulking 6 foot 4 inch Gene Miles, a Broncos captain and a Queensland Origin and Kangaroo legend who played nearly eight years of Test football in the centres and finally at lock, was chairman of the Queensland selectors, and prepared to punt on a young, slight Billy for Queensland's Origin fortunes. Miles had enough knowledge of players from the Far North to know he could rely on Billy's toughness. Miles was born and raised in Townsville, part of the football culture Billy's relatives and father had come out of. A North Queenslander was more than happy to give another North Queenslander a leg up.

On 27 April, Slater woke to the great news he'd been included in Queensland Origin's twenty-two-man preliminary squad. There was talk he would even take over from Darren Lockyer in the fullback role, with Lockyer moving to the five-eighth position—a role Lockyer had switched to with his club, the Broncos. Lockyer, though, was later ruled out of the first Origin match due to injury and Rhys Wesser was selected as fullback.

Then in May, Billy was named in the full eighteen-man squad for Origin. He'd clearly impressed new coach Michael Hagan at Origin pre-training. Billy's fortunes were on the march again.

Hagan said he'd hardly set eyes on Billy before he'd turned up at Origin training in Brisbane. He was impressed by the twenty-year-old who was carrying some big raps from his first season. Hagan's coaching profile was on the rise too. Queensland had put their faith in him and he'd just taken the Newcastle Knights in 2001 to a premiership. He'd coached greats such as Andrew Johns so he knew what a good talent was.

He was instantly impressed by Billy's enthusiasm. 'In all my time, I have never seen a better trainer or a better communicator in our game,' Hagan said.

It was a huge plaudit coming from someone who had played among the best, including Steve Mortimer at Canterbury—and for someone who hadn't missed a match in five seasons when he later played for the Newcastle Knights. Hagan knew about sustained fitness and effort and longevity.

Hagan was pleased with his young charges. All the young men were performing up to expectations, just like experienced Origin players. 'I suddenly had a whole heap of Queensland talent in front of me,' Hagan remembers.

Not that Queensland was awash with debutantes (four); New South Wales had more: six. The Blues were reeling from a pre-season scandal after Mark Gasnier and Anthony Minichiello were sacked for misbehaviour and New South Wales had to call in new talent.

During the Blues' Origin camp, Mark Gasnier was accused of using Anthony Minichiello's phone to make an obscene phone call to a woman outside the Coogee Bay Hotel as seven players decided they would kick on at the Sydney Casino and some at a brothel. A twenty-seven-year-old woman, only known as Melanie, complained of receiving an obscene message from Gasnier, in which he'd urged her to 'fire up' among other lewd suggestions. She made the complaint to radio announcer Ray Hadley on 2GB and sent him the recording of the call. Australian Rugby League chief Geoff Carr initially denied his players had been involved, but after Hadley played him the tape he had no choice but to admit it was one of the Blues players, and later admitted there were two voices on the tape. Gasnier admitted he made the call and later apologised to the woman. He said he'd been under the influence of alcohol when he made the call.

The NSW camp was also thrown into chaos when members of the public reported to the media seeing some

Blues players travelling on a public bus early the next morning, allegedly returning from a brothel owned by well-known punter and league enthusiast Eddie Hayson.

It was a dramatic start to the Origin series before a pass had been made. The Maroons looked on as the New South Wales team was falling apart.

Hagan and his Blues counterpart Phil Gould were at each other even before the players had run on the field for Origin game one. Gould questioned possible go-slow tactics on the field and said the Blues were ready to start a fight if the game descended into farce. He also claimed Smith might use the grapple tackle.

A former Storm player Brett O'Farrell later claimed in 2008 that during the 2004 pre-season Storm players were taught to do the grapple tackle—an illegal, dangerous tackle—and in one instance, an instructor rendered him unconscious with the tackle, a crab-like hold on the back of an opposing player. The Storm were also later accused of using a chicken wing tackle on players in a bid to slow down the play (a player's arm would be pulled back in a tackle to slow down their momentum).

Bellamy fiercely denied his team had been taught to do the grapple tackle. 'Please. I'm telling you that's a load of crap,' Bellamy told the press in 2008. 'I might have said "why didn't you put this hold on him or why didn't you try and turn him on his back there—or why didn't you grip tighter here or why couldn't you grab some handles up here." But when the grapple thing all blew up and came to a head then we were really aware of not doing that sort of stuff.'

Sharp also denies the grapple technique was used on the field, or that there had been any training for it in 2004. 'The Storm just had great defensive plays,' he said.

The Storm had worked on slowing the play down through their tackling techniques. They had employed wrestler John Donehue to teach them techniques in defensive play. This training had been going on all during the 2004 pre-season. Lance was in charge of the Storm's defence coaching.

Lance's view was that slowing the opposition play down meant the Storm were able to get back to the 10 metres defensive line more easily and quickly to avoid possible penalties for off-side. It also disrupted opposition momentum and swayed things the Storm's way by the third ruck:

> We started a wrestling program and we worked with John Donehue. He also worked in the top echelons of jiu-jitsu and grappling. A lot of the boys would end up with cuts and bruises just from the wrestling section of the program. We just wanted our players to be tough and John became a great friend of ours.
>
> We worked out how we should play the game and it proved successful. It was all about trying to slow the play down so we could get back the 10 metres. We worked on that the best way we could. Often you find that after the first or second rucks you will face some attack or someone trying to break your line by the third ruck. We just found ways to nullify that movement in the other team. And we just did the opposite when in attack.

Donehue was a black belt in the Brazilian martial art of jiu-jitsu, a discipline which has an emphasis on holds, grappling and ground fighting. Other sporting teams, including AFL teams, used him to help improve wrestling techniques.

The Age's Mark Fuller said from his observation 'everything Craig Bellamy was about was to try and slow the opposition down'.

'They spent a lot of time trying that out. By and large they didn't do anything illegal. They were doing some grapple tackles or their like but it probably wouldn't have been an issue if it had been any other team than the Storm. There seemed to be campaigns from other clubs which didn't support what was actually happening on the field.'

Controversy was never far from Origin games. Queensland's Hagan hit back at claims the Storm players may use grapple techniques in Origin, saying he knew referee Sean Hampstead would make sure everyone stayed within the rules and would quickly penalise any illegal tackles. Hampstead was in everyone's focus as it was his first Origin match, although he had some experience at senior level, having refereed two Test matches.

Miles was confident the new Queensland young bloods, including Billy, would shine: 'We tried a lot of new combinations [for Origin 2004] and one of those was to put Billy on the wing,' he said. 'We were going through a transition period. We were very well situated for wingers prior to that, with Wendell Sailor and Lote Tuqiri out on the wing. But we didn't have the big 6-foot or more and 15-stone men anymore to put out on the wing. We put Billy out there and he handled it great.'

But the series was a huge baptism of fire for young Billy. He'd go from a good solid start in game one, to the hero and man-of-the-match in game two, to the man-under-pressure by game three. And all in the middle of turning twenty-one.

On 26 May, Billy ran on to Telstra Stadium in front of a rabid Blues crowd, wearing the unfamiliar number five jersey, the 142nd player for Queensland in the modern Origin series. He'd never played at the stadium before, the Olympic stadium, nor had he ever been there. Billy's hair had grown back to almost shoulder length and he looked like a younger version of his dad at the same age. NSW started like a bull out of the gate, three tacklers running heavily into the Queensland players, stunning them in the opening minutes with their ferocious tackling. Billy didn't get his first touch until the third minute.

Billy didn't make a tackle in the first eight minutes and was suddenly under pressure from a nicely weighted New South Wales kick, and took the ball on the full behind the Storm goal line. Commentator Paul 'Fatty' Vautin said the catch would do the young man's confidence a world of good. 'First test of the night for Billy Slater,' Ray 'Rabbits' Warren said. 'Well taken by Billy Slater, that will help his confidence,' Vautin added.

NSW weren't able to convert their early dominance in the play. Billy just missed grounding the ball for a try in the twentieth minute as he followed through a kick into the Blues in-goal. Then Scott Prince scored in the twenty-third minute to put Queensland in the lead despite the Blues' mammoth run of possession. At one stage, Wesser dropped the ball and an eager Billy was on hand to pick up the crumbs before NSW could pounce on the ball near the Maroon line. He was slowly and confidently putting himself into the play. But his tackling technique needed refining: he flew in around the mid-riff of ball-carriers, and more often than not was brushed off. He'd quickly scoot back to the defensive line, eagerness all over his face. Billy seemed lost on the left wing, often only looking on as the battle raged up the middle. It wasn't his normal game: he was a hunter, not an observer.

Billy's birthday chum Cameron Smith (both born on 18 June 1983) was already acting like an Origin veteran in just his second Origin game. Comfortable and in command, Smith was directing play and his precise passing was putting plenty of Maroon players into gaps. He made twenty-six tackles just in the opening half. Smith would continue that relentless effort through his whole career.

The second half started disastrously for the Blues as Hornby and Wing failed to communicate and ran into each other, knocking the ball on from the Storm kick off. But Timmins made up for the embarrassment just six minutes later with a try.

Billy took another high kick at the back. 'There might have been a question about Billy Slater under the high ball but he's answered it beautifully tonight,' fellow Channel Nine commentator Peter Sterling said. Brent Tate went over for a try in the sixty-third minute to make the score 8–8 and the game was headed for an exhilarating finish. Billy almost scored a sensational runaway try as he chimed in perfectly to take, then pass, from Maroon captain Shane Webcke but was ruled off side by the touch judge. Billy had his pants ripped in the process by a diving Blues player vainly trying to grab him. 'He was away Slater,' declared Vautin.

New South Wales had a penalty late in the game right on the Queensland line, but Gould sent out the instruction to kick for goal and then Fitzgibbon missed the subsequent attempt by a whisker. It was a relentless struggle where the debutantes quickly put on the armour of tried warriors and didn't let the crowd of 68,344 screaming league fans down. In the last throw of the game Billy took down fellow debutante Luke Lewis over the line and the two traded stiff looks (they would later become great buddies and Billy would even buy a python off him). Billy had the last play in normal time when a line drop-out came straight to him, and he did the only thing he could do with seconds left—have a shot for a field goal—but his attempt was knocked down by Danny Buderus. Origin went into extra time.

It was the first time that the golden point had come into play since its introduction in 2003, and Timmins, who'd only scored one field goal before in his first class career, thumped the winning goal like a professional in the eighty-third minute, from near the halfway mark. It provoked jubilant scenes from the New South Wales bench with coach Phil Gould running onto the field, holding his arms aloft. It seemed a cruel way to end such an absorbing struggle, which had every element of Origin tenacity, excitement and skill.

'What a night, what a drop kick,' 'Rabbits' Warren exclaimed.

Gould said of the match: 'The game was absolutely outstanding. All thirty-four players, the referee, everyone was under the pump and there was never more than a couple of points in it. Everyone was under pressure and everyone stood up. It was an amazing contest.'

The crowd at Telstra Stadium and the million or more who watched the broadcast on TV had seen a feast of football and a glimpse of Billy's brilliance. He'd had a confident start to Origin, hadn't made a mistake, and could even have won the game in the last second if his kick wasn't knocked down. He'd earned the right to stay in the Maroons team for Origin game two 2004.

The Storm were having a better year, constantly moving between fourth and fifth place on the ladder, with a firm grip on a finals spot as the end of the season approached.

But it wasn't the finals that the boys were worried about. Sharp remembers in one dressing room talk, the boys were dreading the arrival of Bellamy's rigorous pre-season training.

'I think it was only June or July and Cronk turned to Smithy and Billy saying "how long to the pre-season?"'

'Only sixteen weeks to go,' Smith said, shaking his head at the prospect of another scorching round of intense training.

Game two of Origin 2004 at Suncorp Stadium in Brisbane was supposed to be a fairytale return for Blues hero Brad Fittler, whom Gould had enticed out of retirement at the age of thirty-two to spearhead the Blues' assault to clinch the series. But instead of 'Freddy' Fittler becoming the hero, 'Billy the Kid' rode into town and stole the limelight. Billy's amazing try became one of his biggest and proudest achievements and was eventually dubbed 'that moment' and celebrated for years as one of the greatest Origin tries.

In front of a ground-record crowd of 52,478 mainly vocal Queenslanders, Billy ran onto the ground confident of his new role at the top level of the sport. He was just two days out from turning twenty-one. Lockyer was back in the team and ready to give Queensland the inspiration they needed to get back into Origin contention. Billy was still in the wing in the number five jersey.

Queensland were playing catch-up with NSW from the start despite the huge support behind them. At half-time the Blues led 12–6. Billy had seen 2 tries scored on his wing and he felt under pressure and ready to pull something out of the hat when the second half started. In the sixty-second minute, Queensland were down 12–10 when *that* moment happened.

Billy dearly wanted to set the ledger straight after seeing 2 tries scored down his side by the Blues. When Lockyer had the ball just before the half-way mark, Billy wasn't even on the wing. He was running like he always did, as an interventionist fullback, ready and eager to get the ball, his natural game—the free-running kid from Innisfail. Lockyer dropped the ball onto his left foot and within a flash Billy had run through and re-gathered. Billy speared right, swaying and jigging, creating uncertainty in the mind of Blues fullback Anthony Minichiello, carrying the ball like it was a toy or on a string. Then he surprised everyone by toeing the ball over

Minichiello's head the opposite way and darted back left, regathered and dived over the line. It was the kind of chip and chase he'd done down on Goondi Bend maybe hundreds of times when he was a kid. In fact, he used to do it so often when practising with his mates in Innisfail they got sick of it and shouted 'don't kick the bloody ball, Billy'. But he did kick the ball and chased it, and kicked it precisely and accurately on the biggest rugby league stage on earth.

The Channel Nine commentators were floored by Billy's show of skill. Ray 'Rabbits' Warren said it was one of the best Origin tries, while Paul 'Fatty' Vautin declared it 'was one of the greatest Origin tries you will ever see'. 'Absolute brilliant stuff, only a kid with that genius and speed could do that, brilliant stuff,' Vautin exclaimed. Peter Sterling enthused 'this is a kid only a few years ago who was riding track work and now he is one of the most exciting younger players in our game.'

Lockyer later said:

> I can't remember if Billy asked me to kick it, I told him I was going to kick it, or whether it was just one of those things that felt right. Billy was just screaming at the line at speed but whether it was a call or an instinctive thing for both of us, I'm not sure. All I know is that I did my bit and then it was all Billy. I remember when Billy took off and picked it up, I had a rear vision of it all and I thought 'Oh my God, he's going to kick this.' It's one of those plays that very rarely come off. But with each moment— Billy picking up the first kick and then kicking again—

with each moment the roar just got louder and louder. It will go down as one of the greatest Origin tries.

Slater said later he was fired up before his famous try. 'All of a sudden I had a couple of tries scored down my edge. (Tahu had run around Billy to score in the corner and get NSW on the board.) Coming out from half-time I knew I had to step it up and try to get that four points back.'

'The atmosphere at Suncorp was amazing, something I'd never experienced before,' Billy later told MSN. 'I was just a young guy and the talk was about Freddy Fittler coming back for NSW.'

Fittler added later: 'But it was a young kid, a fast kid for Queensland that stole the show.' Perhaps tongue-in-cheek, Fittler added: 'I still think he got through very quick, probably off-side.'

Indeed referee Hampstead wasn't sure and sent the try upstairs to be reviewed by the video referees Tim Mander and Graeme West. They decided the winger had been in line with Lockyer. Steve Mascord reported for *The Sydney Morning Herald* that Blues hooker Danny Buderus kept firing at Hampstead: 'He was offside, he was offside.' But Hampstead replied: 'I'm not the video referee. They ruled him onside.'

There were only inches in it, but in the end Billy was given the benefit of the doubt and the try was awarded.

Blues fullback Minichiello was flummoxed by the quick attack of Billy: 'He tried to take me on the outside, albeit at full pace, but then chipped it back to his left and obviously it was the perfect chip. It bounced right up for him and he scored a great try.'

NSW's Brett Finch said it was 'one of the greatest Origin moments of all time' and all he had seen was a flash of Maroon go flying past him.

Lockyer credits Slater for backing himself. 'He was always talented and willing to take a risk so when you've got that confidence...he was happy to have a crack,' Lockyer said. 'Fortune favours the brave and away he went.'

Ronnie Slater later reflected, in his larrikin way, that he'd seen Billy score a better try: 'I thought the first try he scored that game was the best,' he said. 'The first try he beat three defenders with the ball in his hands. He ran around Anthony Minichiello. The second try he didn't beat anyone with the ball.'

After his great try, Billy sent Timana Tahu over the sideline in the corner to stop a try and a Blues revival. He recovered from an impossible position to tackle Tahu and make him lose the ball just as he was about to put the pill down. It was a match-winning tackle, following a match-winning try.

Everything was turning to gold for Billy. He'd not only scored a try that everyone would hail as one of the best in Origin, certainly in the top five, if not number one, he was named man-of-the-match and Queensland held on to win the game 22–18.

Billy had, it seemed, cemented his place in the Maroons team. Phil Gould said his players played poorly and only had themselves to blame. He called for Hampstead's sacking from game three for a bungled tackle count. 'He's had his shot,' Gould said. Hampstead was later replaced by Paul Simpkins for game three.

Billy was the toast of Queensland, especially Innisfail. It all coincided with his twenty-first birthday celebrations. He was supposed to have a private party at night with family and friends celebrating his coming of age at the Garradunga Community hall, a joint party with his cousin, but his arrival back in Innisfail turned into a community-wide Billy fest.

Innisfail jeweller Elsa Day heard Billy was in town and quickly rounded up some business support and the backing of Johnstone Shire Council to give Billy a grand welcome. Mrs Day got on the phone to Judy Slater to see if Billy would be part of a street celebration and she said 'no worries'. All the logistics were hastily organised and people were lined up three deep on the main street as Billy was driven along amongst the crowd (put at more than 4000).

Girls chanted 'Billy Billy' from the side of the streets and even the checkout girls from Woollies wore 'Go Billy' badges. Originally Billy was supposed to be driven around town in an old ute, but real estate agent George Villaris offered up his own BMW convertible, with an attractive blonde to drive the car. Villaris might have thought a bit more about it later because the surging crowd caused some minor damage to his car including a broken antenna and scratches on his bonnet and side, such was the wild enthusiasm from the Innisfail people to see Billy. Billy's welcome home was almost bigger than the town's annual Harvest Festival.

Billy stopped to talk to young Innisfail Brothers football players by the road and told them: 'Keep going. Chase your dreams. I didn't have any clubs chasing me when I was playing here. I went to Brisbane and played for Norths and went from there to the Storm.'

When Johnstone mayor Neil Clarke presented the keys of the town to Billy, he told the crowd that when he saw Billy play as a youngster he thought there were five or six players who were more likely than him to play top grade football. Clarke knew the Slaters, three generations of them, and he had been course announcer at the rugby league ground Callendar Park for almost thirty years and had worked with Billy's dad Ronnie. Billy was great friends with Clarke's son Craig from a young age, and he sometimes stayed at the Clarke's house overnight in his late teens if parties went on a little late.

Clarke was never sure Billy would make it into the big time. At one stage he thought Billy's cousin James was the better player. But he said he always noticed a determination, a desire to work hard and a love of footy in Billy. So much so, that from an early age a young Billy always went to bed holding a football in his arms. He slept like that for years, a football was his form of a comfort teddy when he was a kid.

Billy never let the adulation go to his head. He was always just one of the boys when he came home. But this day he was getting writer's cramp signing so many autographs.

The procession ended up in Canecutters Court where Clarke said: 'We're proud of Billy and he's obviously proud of us.'

A street party ensued and local federal MP Bob Katter presented an Aussie flag to Billy and flowers to his mum Judy.

Judy was now getting used to being referred to constantly as 'Billy's mum'. Three big birthday cakes were brought out under a bright Innisfail day as Billy got ready for his big birthday bash later that night at the Garradunga Community Hall (right next to the Garradunga Hotel).

But while he was feted in the Far North, Billy was confronted by the reality of living in AFL-mad Melbourne when he returned to Storm headquarters.

As he tried to enter Olympic Park for training, two gatekeepers stopped him because he'd forgotten his pass. 'Are you a player?' one asked. 'Yeah,' Billy said with a big grin on his face.

Origin coach Hagan was keen to see Billy play his normal game, and wanted him to reproduce his exciting burst of play from game two. He was willing to gamble him at some stage in the responsible role at fullback. Some believed he might even take over the fullback role from Wesser, but Billy wasn't sure.

'I don't think Rhys deserves to lose his position,' Slater said. 'He's had a dig in everything he's done in the last couple of games and he's played really good. I'm happy to stay on the wing ... the combination is working really good at the back there and I don't see why you'd change that.'

Billy denied he'd been a match winner in game two, when interviewed by *The Sydney Morning Herald*'s Steve Mascord: 'Match winner? But you've got people out there like Cameron Smith doing forty-five tackles. He's a match winner in my books as well. It's not a one-man effort out there, Shaun Timmins would probably tell you that, too. He won it for them in extra-time but there were another twelve blokes out on that field who busted their arse for the eighty minutes and you just happen to be the one who scores the try.'

Billy was straight back into the thick of things in the NRL competition. Amid the Storm's 42–6 walloping of the Warriors in June he made a 70-metre solo effort to score. Alex Brown wrote in *The Sun-Herald* that Billy again showed 'the mesmeric footwork that highlighted Queensland's stirring victory in Origin II'. And then two weeks later he scored a sensational 100 metre try against the Bulldogs.

Scott Hill said one of Billy's greatest attributes was putting the opposition at sixes and sevens even when he didn't have the ball. As the opposition floundered, not knowing where Billy would fly through next, it often created holes somewhere else for other Storm players to plunder.

Hill said:

> Billy is always looking at opportunities to attack. So that pressure is always on the opposition to try and work out what he is going to do. The opposition player is thinking 'he's going to burn me, so I better get on my bike to stop him'. This often created gaps for us.
>
> What Billy did gave such strength to the halves. And often you'd have three defenders looking out for what Billy was doing because of his pace and ability. He's making the defence move earlier.

Hill said it made his job as a half a lot easier—playing around the wow factor from Billy.

Game three of Origin 2004 would quickly bring Billy back to earth. It would find out what was lacking in his game. Some noted he wasn't willing to take the ball straight up and run hard at the defence, often steering wide. Miles reckons Gould had worked out a strategy and decided to pinpoint Billy at the back and put him under pressure. It was to be the ultimate test for Billy and the lessons he learnt from it would make him one of the best in the game, but in the meantime for a couple of years, he would do it tough.

The big game three of 2004 on 7 July at Telstra Stadium in Sydney was one of the most hyped Origin games in history. Because it was the series decider, marketers did everything in their power to make it the biggest TV event of the year. At its viewing peak, game three would attract 1.284 million viewers throughout Australia to Channel Nine's coverage, the most watched program on TV that year. And Billy's skills were used as one of the big marketing factors for the game. It was almost as big as the Olympics. And there was an Olympic-sized crowd at the stadium to watch it—more than 82,000 league fans. The only downer was that the field was wet and slippery, and this would prove a nightmare scenario for Billy.

It seemed like it was going to be another special night for Billy. He scored the first try and Queensland led 8–0. But from then on things only got worse for Billy and Queensland. He spilled the ball three times in the first twenty minutes and Gould's strategy to pinpoint him was working. Billy was dumped in one of the heaviest tackles you would see, with

Craig Fitzgibbon and Nathan Hindmarsh descending on him and hurling him to the ground on his back. Some said Hindmarsh showed uncharacteristic aggressiveness in the tackle with a raised elbow that almost collected Billy.

(Later, the match review committee looked at the incident but took no action. Committee man Ross Livermore said: 'Hindmarsh was lucky he didn't come down with that elbow, he missed with that,' said Livermore. 'Otherwise it could have been nasty. We thought the referee may have given a penalty for that.')

Most at the time wondered why Billy wasn't given a penalty because it appeared he'd been clearly lifted in the tackle. After Billy spilled the ball again, the Blues went on the offensive launching attack after attack until Mark Gasnier ran inside Billy and Scott Prince to score. The Blues looked unbeatable and led Queensland 18–8 at half-time.

Paul Malone from *The Courier Mail* saw the game and said 'few would have thought Billy Slater, the quicksilver, sure-fingered hero of Queensland's game two win, in line to be a potential culprit in Origin's ultimate tiebreaker.' Malone said Billy's first half performance was 'nightmarish'. 'This was a sobering night of education in which Hagan swung him back to fullback for a short stint in a bid to change the momentum for the under-pressure Maroons. Slater skidded around at times like a first-time ice-skater on the greasy Telstra Stadium surface,' Malone said.

'Slater finished the game and whether he was the worse for wear for the brutal Fitzgibbon tackle was not immediately known. But his carrying of the football in one hand, which has so often seemed an exciting expression of youthful self-confidence, suddenly looked reckless.'

Critics slammed his bad choices in the game, especially when he missed a tackle on a rampant Gasnier.

It was the total opposite of game two. In the last play of the game, Fittler ran in to block a Lockyer kick, knocked it down, recollected the ball and ran away to score, creating his fairytale ending in his last Origin game. New South Wales ran out winners 36–14. It had been a giant of a series with more than 200,000 people attending the three games of Origin, an all-time record.

It was a brute test of strength as well, that left Gasnier on the sidelines for a month with a collarbone injury and Queenslander Matt Sing with a double jaw fracture and nerve damage. (Incredibly, Sing came back at end of the season for the finals, scoring 3 tries against the Bulldogs for the Cowboys.)

Miles's biggest fear was that Gould would target Billy at the back—and his fears came true. Gould was one of the game's master tacticians and was an expert at targeting weaknesses in the opposition—in this case he tried to show up a young Billy under intense attack.

'The problem was Gould had pinpointed him and Billy got terribly man-handled. He had two or three guys bearing down on him and he was "rag-dolled" by the Blues. They dumped him on his back and really gave it to him.'

'Billy probably now realises, and it's a terrible lesson to learn, that State of Origin is a hell of a game,' Miles said.

'He had his own fairytale in game two, but it ended that night [in Origin three]. He had a twenty-first birthday, a ticker tape parade and signed a million autographs after the second game. But the rude reality is you have to get up for these games and, hopefully, he realises that now.'

Billy agreed he had to learn from his mistakes, and wanted to jump straight back on the horse in the Storm's match the following Sunday:

> You definitely look forward to the next week after you have a bad game, so I'll be looking to have a big one on Sunday.
>
> If I have a bad game I try not to hide and make excuses for myself. I think the only way to learn is to own up and take note of your mistakes. I've done that, and I'm going to be working on my ball security. Hopefully it can make me a better player for my club, and hopefully I can take a little bit of leadership back into the Storm and improve my game a couple of notches.

The 2004 season ended in finals misery for the Storm, again losing to the Bulldogs, this time 43–18 in the semi-final. But Billy's season in 2004 had already come to a grinding halt. The Storm's fullback was out of gas just as the finals approached, carrying a groin injury. Bellamy lamented his young charge wasn't turning up for training and hoping to get by with just a small training session on the Friday before the game. 'My big concern is that, over the next five or six years, Billy isn't going to develop into the player he is capable of being unless we can get this right. It is no good Billy turning up to training on a Friday with the team and then playing on the weekend.'

Bellamy reckoned Billy was only performing at 65 per cent of his potential. He'd been carrying the injury almost from the time he started playing in the Storm's first grade side. Billy had osteitis pubis, an inflammation of the pelvic area where the right and left pubic bones meet, a painful condition that sometimes afflicts long distance runners, footballers, dancers and ice skaters.

Billy had to curtail his running and confine most of his training to ball work, cycling, boxing and weightlifting. He had hardly done any pre-season training with the team and by August he'd run into a fitness crisis as the season progressed after the demanding Origin series and NRL competition took his body to the brink.

He admitted the injury was causing him great pain, but he hadn't been having injections to ease the symptoms. Billy possibly faced a long time on the sidelines. It came to a head when the Storm played the Dragons in early August and he was taken off the field. Storm doctor Michael Makdissi hoped they could manage the injury for the rest of the season. But Billy's best option was to rest.

Doctors said the injury had been there for about eighteen months. A CAT scan and X-ray confirmed the injury after the Dragons game, in which the Storm were walloped.

'It has been getting a little bit worse towards the end of the season but that is to be expected. Obviously I am doing a little bit more running and that is catching up on me,' Slater said at the time.

A team of Storm and sports medical experts were drawn upon to choose a course of action as the end of 2004 neared.

It was decided Billy would undergo surgery through a well-known Newcastle specialist Dr Neil Halpin, who had done many surgical operations on injured footballers—more than 4000 specifically on osteitis pubis.

The operation involved two cuts to the side of the groin area to release the pressure. Surgery was not necessarily a sure cure for Billy, but fate was on his side. The rate of full recovery for elite athletes after surgery for osteitis pubis was extremely high and Billy showed immediate signs of improvement.

Billy had ended the season unsure how the injury would leave his game. But his fortunes would change dramatically the next year.

CHAPTER SIX

A ROSE FOR BILLY

If Billy's life was all about football, it was perhaps a little surprising that the new great passion in his life knew very little about football. But maybe that was a perfect alignment of Yin and Yang. Nicole Rose was an early friend from Billy's gymkhana days when they had hung out together with all their horse-loving mates. Billy was at Innisfail pony club and Nicole was at Freshwater pony club. They'd ride at horse meets together on weekends and share the thrills and spills on the Far North riding circuit. They'd met as youngsters at ages eleven and thirteen and knew each other into their later teens. An affection was always there between the two and that grew over the years.

Nicole was a Cairns girl with a lot of get up and go. She started her own art business without any art lessons. Her father, Nick, who worked in the Royal Australian Navy, had built a special studio for her to paint in, and she loved it with all her heart. Nicole and her father were very close. Nicole spent much of her time pushing doors open in Cairns to sell her works. They were colourful pieces that evoked the lushness of the Far North tropics.

A set of circumstances meant Billy was in Cairns early in the year for a trial game against the Cowboys in February. He had Nicole's number and decided to give her a ring while he was in town. She didn't know he played for the Melbourne Storm or that he had scored *that* try. She just remembered him as a happy, good-looking young man she had met all those years ago, with a shared love of horses.

Nicole was everything Billy could wish for. She was a bright, vivacious girl with a big, wide smile and an easy going North Queensland manner. Nicole would provide the perfect foil for him away from the heady life of football. Because of their shared interest in the outdoors and horses, they could dream of a life after football as well. They'd often talk of eventually owning a bit of land to run a horse-riding business. The love would blossom during the year, but Nicole would stay in Cairns for the time being.

Nicole told *The Sunday Mail*: 'I knew he went away but didn't know he was playing football. I had no idea he was this "superstar". He gave me a call and we went to a local waterfall together and things kind of went from there.'

Billy turned from his new love back to concentrate on his football for the important trial in the Far North, which was really almost a home game for him.

In the trial in Cairns on 25 February, Melbourne Storm scored 24 unanswered points in the second half to overrun

North Queensland 30–18. Billy was one of the try-scorers. It was a momentous visit to Queensland for the Storm—and for Billy. The Storm also defeated the Broncos in an earlier trial game on the Gold Coast.

Billy was still finding his feet after his injury and enjoyed the star treatment back in Queensland. He visited Longreach as part of an NRL promotional program. He admitted every time he came back to Queensland it was 'pretty full-on'.

Billy and his Storm buddies Dallas Johnson and Steve Bell were mobbed by students from Longreach State School. But they only wanted to know about Billy. Bell was used to the adulation for Billy. Once, on a dance floor, two women appeared to be staring at Bell and he thought 'mmm, I've still got it'. Then he realised they were looking at someone behind him—Billy.

Billy told a reporter in Melbourne later: 'You feel like a rock star but after a couple of days of that you can get sick of it. It can sort of get to you a little bit, so being in Melbourne is great, you can get away from football and go and have a game of golf and no-one will even know who you are and people will treat you like an everyday person.'

Billy was happy to be out and about after working around his injury for so many months, often having to put ice bags on his legs after every game to ease the pain.

'That was one of the frustrating things about last year with the injury. It wasn't so much what you did on the field it was what you couldn't do off the field,' Slater told *The Age*'s Stathi Paxinos. 'If you had a bad game in defence you couldn't get out there during the week and practise that or go out and practise under the high ball, you just had to back up on the weekend.'

Billy was on the mend. His groin surgery had been a success and he was now almost back to full training.

Bellamy said Billy was training at an 'excellent level'. 'It was tough for him to maintain fitness last year,' Bellamy said. 'Basically, we didn't see him at training until our final session of the week. He's had the surgery and if he keeps going the way he's been going at training, he's in for a big year. It's a bit mind-boggling how good he could be.'

Billy was confident he'd seen the back of the niggling problem:

> It was only minor surgery but it has helped me a lot. I'm moving really well and I'm excited about the season ahead. It got pretty bad in the end. It was difficult to maintain my fitness levels and it showed a bit on the field. I ran a bit before Christmas and, since we came back from the break, I haven't missed a session. I'm feeling much fitter and, hopefully, that means I can look for chances a bit more. We have some great ball players and I want to offer them as much support as I can.

Luckily, Billy had missed the most intense part of pre-season training instituted by Bellamy, which he now reserved mostly for new recruits. Players were taken away to a camp in coastal western Victoria, where they were confronted mentally and physically. It was so tough some of them bled from the effects of sand chafing their legs as they ran up and down sand dunes. Some just wanted to leave straight away. The training was hosted by ex-army officers from the special operations group. It was like Bellamy was getting ready to put players into battle.

Storm centre Steve Bell was one of many who went through Bellamy's extreme camp. It was usually held just before Christmas—not much of a Christmas present for the players.

Bell remembers the ex-army officers placed the players into different coloured shirts and gave each one a number:

> We couldn't talk to each other, but just yell out 'yellow one' or 'blue two'. We did uphills, downhills, push-ups, every type of exertion.
>
> After a hard day of training we were told to make up tents for that night and we thought 'here we go, finally some rest', but when we went to go to bed they said 'those are not for you they are for us [the trainers], you're sleeping over there'. We looked over and there was nothing but a bunch of rags on the ground in the open. They did some cruel things to us.
>
> Some people got something out of it. Mostly it was showing how we could lead by example to all the other players.

Bell remembers at every training session Billy was always at the forefront, always pushing the barriers. Bell was from Emerald in Queensland and went through the same feeder system of Norths Devils in Brisbane to the Storm in Melbourne. He was one of Norths' best ever players—a big statement considering the league royalty that went through there—scoring 45 tries in the Queensland Cup competition before he headed south.

Bell said Billy was always vocal. 'He was always cheeky, but just friendly banter, he was never quiet. But one thing I know he was no good at speeches at parties, especially at Ryan Hoffman's twenty-first.'

Bell believes Billy's love of surfing helped him get over his groin injury.

Bell was unusual in the higher ranks. He didn't have a full-time manager. His manager was Wade Fenton—the player from Norths Billy had shared a house with for a short time. Fenton's contract with Bell was just based on a handshake. Such loyalty was a rarity in the modern game.

The Storm was settling well into its place in Melbourne amongst the AFL minions. Melburnians were even tuning in to watch the State of Origin matches. They saw players like Cronk, Crocker, Johnson, Smith, Inglis and Billy representing the Storm as much as Queensland, so State of Origin became an attractive viewing proposition.

(Greg Inglis joined the ranks of the Storm in 2005. He would start in a quiet manner, playing just thirteen games, but the next year his talent would explode and he would become a try-scoring machine for the Storm and also gain Origin selection for Queensland. He was a natural fullback but Billy's class would keep him out of that position until he left the Storm and joined the Rabbitohs in 2011 following the salary cap crisis. Until then he would play a utility role in the Storm's backline.)

Reporter Mark Fuller was able to get into the bunker of the Storm during his six years of reporting on rugby league for *The Age*, owned by Fairfax. *The Age* treated the Storm's arrival in town as it would for any AFL-mad area, as a minor sport, while the News Limited owned opposition, *Herald Sun*, went over the top to promote the Storm. Fuller, though, said he didn't feel left out in the cold by the News Limited franchise, and although he missed a few heads-ups on stories, he felt he was given access to the Storm whenever he wanted it. He got on well with the Storm's early public relations manager Chris 'Apples' Appleby.

Fuller believes the team was given a huge kick along by the early secure administration of Ribot and Chris Johns. The team hit a rough patch in the early 2000s, but gathered momentum under Bellamy and with the influx of new talent including Billy.

He noted the Storm had a knack of picking up players who were out on the edge or had been overlooked by other NRL teams—players such as Matt King, who was working in a bar before he was spotted by the Storm, who went on to become a huge part of the team.

The essence of the Storm motto was to sign players who could adapt to life in Melbourne and would not go stir-crazy and run off the rails. They wanted talented players with strong character.

Johns backs up Fuller's view: 'With a new club we just had to get the best people. Not just anyone, they had to be good people. Billy was one of those. He was hardworking, hungry to play and had a fire in his belly. But the thing was that Billy wanted to play for us [the Storm]. It was the club that was attracting him to come.'

Fuller's access to Bellamy was limited. Despite Bellamy's outbursts during a game where he would be screaming down the microphone to his sideline eye Dean Lance, Fuller said Bellamy was generally 'quite shy'. 'I think with Craig, he just wanted to get on with the job. He wasn't about cultivating a relationship with the media,' Fuller said. Fuller had the impression the Storm were always looked down on by the other league clubs, especially in Sydney.

> You often had the feeling they wanted to kill off the Storm. They seemed to be jealous of the Storm's early success.
>
> Ribot had to do all the hard yards and there was no sympathy there from the other NRL clubs or from the AFL. It was always hard for Ribot trying to sign up top players. He felt the club should be treated just as Brisbane and Sydney were in the AFL, with special concessions to attract players. I think the fact this never happened always frustrated him. The club probably started thinking 'well stuff them, we'll just get on with it'. I'm sure it was the genesis of what happened with the salary cap crisis.

Fuller said Billy had set the place on fire with his first couple of games:

> Just the sheer pace of the guy was outstanding and one of the amazing things was when the Storm were back

on their own line defending someone would grubber through a kick, Billy would pounce on it at full speed. Other fullbacks would just hold the ball or sit on it. He had the self-belief he could pick up the ball and run away. Sometimes he'd suddenly have Melbourne right back on the attack or even run away for a length of the field try. He did that right from the start of joining the Storm.

Fuller said the Storm concentrated on having the best players in the number nine, seven and one jumpers. 'It was the same all along, they had a top hooker in Richard Swain, then he left and they got Smith, they had Kimmorley at halfback, then they got Cronk, they had Ross, and then they got Slater. That was a very important part of the Storm mindset, the best at nine, seven and one.'

The Storm started the year with a bang. They had big wins against the Knights and the Dragons in the first two rounds and were leading the competition after piling on ninety-four points in two games.

Billy scored 3 tries in the first game of the year, putting behind him any fears about his injury. He ruined the comeback of Newcastle's Andrew Johns after Johns was out of the game for twelve months through injury. Billy was the man of the match and in one of his 3 tries he replicated his famous Origin moment with another chip and chase to score. The Storm smashed Newcastle 48–10 at Olympic Park and it was an emphatic start to the season. (Johns would get his revenge later in the season when Newcastle defeated the Storm 37–18, with Johns, not Billy, starring.)

There was talk early in the year that Billy might earn an Australian jumper for the Anzac Test. He missed out and instead he was off playing in the nation's capital against a depleted Raiders team, hoping to keep up the Storm's tradition of beating them under Bellamy. Billy had an awesome game, scoring 2 tries and having a big hand in 2 other tries as the Storm overran Canberra 46–10 in late April. Lance was on hand to oversee the game with Bellamy away on Test duties. He felt Billy and two other storm players, Orford and King, should have been given a Test jumper.

'They were obviously unlucky, and it's a very good way to show they are still around,' Lance said after the game. 'Billy, in particular, was just outstanding today, he was very scary.'

Billy's chances of playing in the first Origin game were given a shake when he was charged with head-slamming Cronulla winger David Simmonds in round six when the Sharks defeated the Storm 30–10. Billy put in an early guilty play in the hope he would get a short suspension. He was charged with grade two contrary conduct. He decided to go with the guilty plea after watching the incident on video. Slater said:

> We've got the bye this week and, with the Origin coming up, if I contested it and didn't succeed, it meant I wouldn't be eligible for the first Origin.
>
> I saw it on video and I took the one week. I definitely don't go out there to break rules or intentionally hurt someone. It's not part of my game. I very rarely tackle much.

> It's just one of the things where Cam [hooker Cameron Smith] lifted his legs up and my arm sort of came across the head, so I'm just going to take the one week and get on with my football. It was something where I got into a position where I accidentally hurt someone. It's just one of those things ... It's something I have to put behind me now and [I will] work hard over the next couple of weeks at training and get back on the field.

If Billy thought he was to be targeted in the upcoming Origin series, he was right. It was the biggest risk for Queensland. Would Stuart (Ricky Stuart was the New South Wales coach, replacing Gould) send his Blues henchmen into battle to knock over Billy again? One headline before Origin blared 'Origin trump Slater used to being target'. The article went on to say that Billy was unconcerned by claims Blues players would target him in the Origin opener. It followed a warning delivered in mid-April by Parramatta forward Nathan Hindmarsh that part of the Eels' plan to beat Melbourne was to hit Slater hard in defence early in the match to put Slater off his game. The ploy worked as the Storm were defeated by Parramatta 26–14. There was no doubt the Blues were ready to do the same to Billy in Origin 2005.

Chris Johns had the inside knowledge of what New South Wales were up to. Although he seemed more of a Queenslander than a New South Welshman, having been born in Queensland, Johns later played his first Origin qualifying games as a young player in New South Wales. He was a star player at the Broncos for nine years and a stalwart of the club and then the Super League bid. But he'd represented New South Wales between 1989 and 1994. After his stint as Storm chief executive—where he helped create the club culture that continues to this day—he left and set up his own successful car-washing business (Hoppy's Handwash Café) with Aussie cricket hero Ian Healy in Brisbane.

In the 2004 series Johns was the NSW team manager. He was in charge of the team when a bonding session among Blues players at Coogee went horribly wrong. It resulted in two players being axed and five fined. Johns offered to resign because he accepted the blame for not telling Blues players to stay at their Coogee hotel base and not go out on the town after they returned together at 3am from the bonding session. The NSWRL board rejected his offer to resign, but was in free-fall from the bad publicity. He didn't back up for the 2005 Origin series but still went to the Blues' camps as a motivator.

As Origin preparations got back on track, Johns was privy to some of the tactics employed to unsettle Queensland and a lot of it was about unsettling Billy. Gould had targeted Billy, and it looked like Stuart would do the same.

'He [Billy] started to get spotted very heavily. He was one of the most marked players in the game,' Johns said. 'The emphasis was to get to Slater and put as much physical pressure on him as possible—basically hit him as hard as you can. The idea at the camp was that if we can smash Slater out of the game we can negate a lot of their potency.'

Origin was turning into a war of tactics like no other league competition. The Blues thought if they took out one of the opposition's most dangerous weapons in Billy they could win the battle for supremacy. In a sense it was a huge compliment to Billy's talent that he should be the focus of such attention. Origin was a terrible baptism of fire for him, a mammoth test many players would never have got through. He got through it all, though, to the other side, a stronger and better and tougher player. In the end, for nearly six years he would make New South Wales pay and have the last laugh.

As his Storm mate Steve Bell said: 'he copped it hard, but he gave it back as hard as he got.'

'He could throw them [fight],' Bell added.

Johns said Billy attracted one of the most concerted efforts he had seen in rugby league to target a player.

> They [the Blues] put a price on his head and said 'let's put him out of the game'. To his credit he came out of that better, he copped some pretty cheap shots. For someone who was so heavily targeted and such a marked man, that was a big statement. It magnified how tough he is.

Slater appeared nonplussed by the Blues blowtorch. He'd already copped the same in the regular NRL competition.

'They're the same people mate, they're the same people in club level so it doesn't matter what they're going to do,' Billy said. 'I can't worry about what they're going to do, I just have to worry about my own game and if I get that right, I'm sure everything will go all right.'

It was unseasonably warm leading up to game one in Brisbane, providing the perfect environment for the players from the Sunshine State to bloom. In front of a record 52,484 people at Suncorp Stadium, Billy was finally able to run on in the coveted fullback position. He'd beaten the experienced Rhys Wesser and the emerging huge talent of Bronco Karmichael Hunt for the role. Everyone was crossing their fingers he would survive the expected onslaught of Blues tacklers. Hagan had overlooked some disappointing mistakes by Billy in the last game of the 2004 Origin series to give Billy another chance.

'We know they're going to jump the gun and try and get three or four men in on most plays and shut our forward pack down to nullify the likes of Lockyer and Slater and Thurston,' Hagan said. He expected wrestling tactics from the NSW forwards.

Queensland had all the momentum in the first part of the game, leading 13–0 at half-time, and then kept the flow in the second half, rattling up 19 unanswered points. Billy played his part in the great start. After twenty minutes Billy steamed on to a pass from Darren Lockyer and then the ball rebounded forward when he was tackled and his Innisfail-raised mate Ty Williams followed through, smartly extricating the ball from the ground and smashing the ball down for the first try. Referee Paul Simpkins went to the video referee to judge whether the ball had only come off Billy's knee, or had touched his hand as well. Video replays seemed inconclusive, but Williams was given the benefit of the doubt. Smith converted to make it 10–0. Billy had been part of the first points from a penalty when the Blues defence tried to haul him in and were penalised for holding on to him for too long.

New South Wales came back with a vengeance in the second half. Winger Luke Rooney scored after a pass from centre Matt Cooper put him over in the corner in the fifty-second minute. The Blues were on a roll when the two sacked players from the previous year's Origin combined for a try. Blues fullback Anthony Minichiello burst through a Lockyer tackle and his pass put Gasnier over. All was forgiven! The Maroons were under pressure with twelve minutes to go when Cooper kicked infield and Fitzgibbon picked it up and dived over to score. At 19–14, the game was in the balance and then an injured Danny Buderus scored a try after a break by Storm player Matt King. Stuart leapt in the air when Fitzgibbon made it 20–19. There was only three minutes to go and then out of nowhere a young Jonathan Thurston stepped up to Origin history and kicked a field goal to make it 20–20 to take the game into extra time. It was a warning for years to come: Thurston, one of league's greatest talents on the main stage, made a freak play, just as Billy had done the previous year in his rookie Origin series. Queensland was brimming with rising talent.

The game went into extra time and then the magic moment occurred. Cowboys player Matt Bowen snatched the ball out of thin air to intercept a Kimmorley pass, leaving the gutted NSW players looking back as Bowen raced away almost the length of the field for the match-winning try and a game one victory (24–20). The Suncorp crowd went into wild celebrations and again Billy felt like he was on top of the world.

The Storm were again having an indifferent season, even though they were studded with stars. On 5 June, the Storm broke a long running hoodoo by winning for the first time at Leichhardt Oval against the Tigers and 17,000 screaming Balmain fans. But it didn't look good for them at half-time as they trailed 8–0. In the break, Bellamy blasted his players for a string of errors and giving away penalties. Billy copped part of the Bellamy spray.

'He wasn't too happy at half-time, he put a couple of rockets up us,' Slater said. 'The penalties were about 7–2 and he wasn't blaming the ref at all, he said we earned every one of them. It was just a discipline thing and I think we took that on board and played to our strengths, got forward in numbers and worked their big men around the middle a little bit. Once we got one on the board, we got a bit of confidence going and we went on with it.'

Billy scored twice as the Storm ran rampant running in thirty points in the second half, to win 30–14 and leave the Leichhardt faithful deflated. The Storm were struggling to show consistency during the season and were bouncing about between fifth, sixth and seventh spots on the ladder as the competition progressed.

In the next Origin game, Billy got his chance to put New South Wales to the sword and achieve Origin glory—the most prized trophy in football. But it was to be only a tribute to the genius of Andrew Johns. Johns was only just getting into gear after his comeback from a knee reconstruction when he broke his jaw playing for Newcastle against the Warriors two months previously. But he appeared to be in a blue streak of form when he put on his Blues jersey for game two of Origin 2005 on 22 June at Telstra Stadium. He was called in at the last moment after New South Wales lost Kimmorley and Trent Barrett. The game turned into a showcase for the genius of Johns.

Hagan, who'd coached Johns, was only left to lament he wasn't on his team as the prodigious talent tore Queensland apart. Johns and Minichiello combined brilliantly to open the scoring in the fifteenth minute. Billy saw his chance to shine and took it. A failed pass between Minichiello and Anasta led to the ball popping up and, of course, an ever-alert Billy was on the spot to pounce on the ball and speed away for a 70 metre try to give Queensland the lead.

NSW fought back with Johns the destroyer. He made a 40–20 kick and during the subsequent run of play Minichiello scored. Johns also had a big hand in the last try of the game scored by Buderus. New South Wales won 34–22 and the Origin series was again headed to a climactic decider, but this time on Queensland's home turf.

Stuart was ecstatic at Johns' performance: 'He's got the same bearing on Origin football that Wally Lewis had.'

'We're alive now!' Johns declared. 'What a game the third one will be! It's been my dream to come back like this. It's what drove me when I was out with the broken jaw.'

Billy had an uninspiring game, but it seemed he'd done nothing terribly wrong to make his position under pressure.

But his performance suddenly came under the public microscope, some described his effort in game two as 'flat'.

Bellamy backed his star fullback to stay in an Origin jumper, especially after Billy starred in a romp over the Rabbitohs following the Origin.

'It's been a pretty tough couple of weeks for Bill, there's no hiding behind that,' Bellamy said. 'He probably wasn't at his best in Origin and he certainly played quite poorly for the way Billy Slater can play. Certainly he knew he had to go out there and play well for us and get back to being Billy Slater.'

Bellamy said he had pointed out a couple of things to Slater during the week. 'And he went out there and was tremendous,' Bellamy said. 'He got back to what works for him and hopefully they will ... leave him in the Origin side because he deserves to be there.'

Bellamy's pleas, though, fell on deaf ears. The Origin powers were worried. They were searching for the killer blow against the Blues and a rampant Johns. They felt Billy had too many risk sides for the important decider. Bowen had stamped his authority with some great plays and the Queensland selectors went for the Cowboys connection to bolster the Maroons charge.

Slater admitted his support play had fallen away.

But then the bad news came. Billy was out of game three. He was livid and angry and couldn't understand why. Queensland coach Hagan was one of those that had made the decision to drop Billy.

'I was off his Christmas card list for a long time,' said Hagan. 'He did have this odd error in his game, especially in his carry of the ball, Also there were issues under the high ball. Sometimes you have to make hard decisions and you hope the players take the tip. It was a bit of tough love from me and then from Mal [Mal Meninga].' (Mal Meninga took over as Origin coach the next year and also decided to keep Billy out of the Maroons team for 2006.)

Most observers were dumbstruck by the decision. How could such a star be axed? League writer and former coach Roy Masters wrote:

> Queensland has turned on itself. The most parochial state in the nation is angry at the selectors of its favourite sporting team for its latest disloyalty: omitting Billy Slater for the third and deciding State of Origin match tomorrow night in Brisbane.
>
> Slater is loved in Queensland—a natural-born thriller with enough wattage in his smile to relieve Brisbane's overworked power grid. His sacking has prompted many Queenslanders to boycott the game and Innisfail, Slater's home town, to threaten to turn off their TV sets.

Even Billy's old mentor mark Muppet Murray was shaking his head in disbelief. 'The reaction has been hostile in some quarters,' he said.

It appeared the Cowboys factor had ruled everyone's minds. The selectors thought combining Bowen, Thurston and Sing from the Cowboys would give the Maroons solidity.

Graham Murray, coach of the Cowboys, said Billy didn't have a kicking game and backed his Cowboys players, 'whereas Bowen can come in late in the tackle count and take the pressure off the kickers'.

Masters said the omission of Slater had made NSW 'delighted'. 'Slater is a rare talent whose acrobatics, athleticism and speed confuse opponents and thrill crowds as if they were at the circus. Slater's anticipation is the best in the NRL and he has made an art form of running off inside passes. OK, he is error-prone, an inevitability with players who tread the fine line between creative abandon and recklessness.'

'Every time I hear someone say Queensland are crazy for dropping Slater, I remind myself this is what they want you to think,' former Blues player and Storm chief executive Chris Johns told Masters.

Blues Origin hero Andrew Johns was surprised at Billy's dumping and said he was too much of talent to be left out for too long:

> I don't know what their thoughts were. They might be planning to play a style that suits Matty Bowen better. If I try to look into it, I think they'll throw the ball around a lot more and play a lot more second phase, which will bring Bowen into the game. I've got a massive rap on Billy Slater. I feel for him because he's an exceptional player. He'll be back next year. There's something wrong if he's not.

Billy was hurting and Bellamy could see it. 'Sometimes it can be like a death in the family but he's dealt with it really well,' Bellamy said.

Billy was trying to fathom why this had happened. 'It does [feel like a kick in the guts] a little bit,' he said. 'Obviously whenever you get dropped from any side, whether it's a first-grade or a representative side, you do feel a bit of a letdown … It's the last Origin, it's one-all, it's the decider up in Queensland, so I'd really like to be there for this one. But as it happens, I can't be and I've got a year to think about that.'

Players back at the Storm, though, didn't notice any drop off in Billy's enthusiasm for the game. 'Billy's not one to dwell on things like that,' Bell said.

Everyone noted how well Billy had been playing including in the club game against South Sydney, with Billy scoring 3 tries in the 48–6 demolition of the Rabbitohs on 25 June.

'Obviously the South Sydney game had nothing to do with it,' Billy said. 'I was pretty happy with my performance on Saturday night, so obviously it was a decision they made from the two Origins before that.'

Bellamy was shocked:

> I wasn't aware he was under any sort of pressure. As Billy said, he didn't have his happiest game in the second Origin but he wasn't Robinson Crusoe there as far as the Queenslanders go. Matty Bowen is a good player but I really feel for Billy and I don't think he deserved to be left out. But at the same time, where I'm really disappointed for him is to not be playing in front of his home crowd in a deciding third Origin.

Selector Gene Miles reckoned Billy had to learn to take the ball up harder through the ruck. Miles said Billy often steered wide when he should be running straight into the defence. In a sense they wanted Billy to toughen up, he was still only slightly built. He had some growing to do. It was kind of a Queensland tough love, forging a new Billy.

'In Origin you have got to go as hard in the seventy-ninth minute as you do in the first minute,' Miles said.

'Gould had left Billy under no illusions how ferocious it is.'

Hagan said Billy was entitled to feel 'very disappointed' after being dropped from the side. The decision was mainly to do with the symmetry of Bowen at fullback with his Cowboy teammates in the backs. 'The fact that he [Bowen] does play with Ty Williams and Matty Sing, and also Johnathan Thurston, I guess there's that understanding they have together,' he said. 'But I think Billy could be feeling very disappointed and I know that he wasn't all that happy when I spoke to him.'

Whether it was a stupid move or wise move, no-one will know. Game three was a one-act affair for New South Wales on 6 July anyway, Billy or no Billy, with Johns again shining and Billy's Storm buddy Matt King scoring 3 tries for the Blues to help NSW win the decider 32–10 and stun the Suncorp Stadium crowd.

It was the last time New South Wales would win an Origin series for nine years. Billy would be part of the dominating force of Queensland players, but he would have to cool his heels for a while.

The Storm finished the season in sixth place and played Brisbane in the qualifying final at Suncorp on 10 September. The Storm were on top early but the Broncos fought back. The score was 18–10 in the sixty-second minute when Billy slipped over picking up the ball at the back and tore ligaments in his ankle. He was taken off the field and later found to have 'torn fibres of the ligaments that run between the tibia and fibula, just above the ankle joint, as well as some of the fibres of the lateral ligament of the ankle', according to the Storm's physio Mary Toomey. Slater would be forced out for at least six weeks.

His loss gave the chance for a young rookie to make his first display of his brilliance in finals football. Greg Inglis had only filled in for Billy for five minutes as fullback when the eighteen-year-old took a pass from Orford and crossed near the goalposts untouched.

Orford's conversion took the Storm's lead to 24–12. A late try by the Broncos proved too late. It was the second time in two years the Storm had beaten Brisbane in a final on Brisbane's home ground.

Billy was sure Inglis could step up to the plate for the big semifinal against the Cowboys after Billy was ruled out. 'If there's someone who could fill my spot, then Greg's the man. He's proven it in the past and he's a great young player, so I'm sure he'll do well,' Billy said.

But the Storm missed Billy. They were beaten 24–16 and missed their chance for a grand finals berth in a lacklustre display. It was the third time in three years they had been kicked out of the finals in the second round. The Storm almost stole a win despite the Cowboys looking the better team, but a try by the Cowboys four minutes from the end stopped a Storm comeback and sealed the victory at the Sydney Football Stadium.

It was a disappointing year for the Storm; crowds at Olympic Park had dwindled over the course of the year. And the team received almost no coverage on Channel Nine in Melbourne, with any replays late at night alongside infomercials. Also, three major players were leaving—Bell, Orford and Kearns (although Kearns would stay in an administrative role at the Storm).

Bellamy said his side lacked the will to win when the going got tough. He nominated 2006 as a rebuilding year. He hoped the likes of Cronk, Smith, King, Johnson and Billy would step up and re-invigorate the Storm.

Billy's year ended in injury again. But there was one good thing to come out of it. Nicole agreed to join him in Melbourne and they would start a new life together and plan a family. She would provide the support that would help him get his career back on track. In the meantime it was back to the gym for Billy to help rebuild his strength. He started working overtime rebuilding his body and increasing his upper body strength, determined to show those Queensland selectors he was made of hard stuff. He had ended the year again as the biggest try scorer for the Storm and there were a lot of positives amongst the debris.

CHAPTER SEVEN

ANNUS HORRIBILIS

The Storm were under pressure as the 2006 season kicked off with pundits saying they would struggle without Kearns, Orford and Bell. The signing of Michael Crocker from the Sydney Roosters, though, strengthened the Storm pack and its tackling prowess.

Bellamy had been on the players' case from early on. From November the previous year, he had made the Storm train the house down, with the annual army camp also beefing up proceedings. The Storm also did some pre-season cross-training with North Melbourne.

It was the chance for Cooper Cronk to show his abilities. He'd been in the shadow of Orford for the previous season but now had the opportunity to become a playmaker on the big stage at halfback.

Cronk was confident he could pick up where Orford had left off. He denied the Storm would struggle in 2006 and that all the players including Smith and Billy would stand up for a great season. His prediction would prove correct.

'Matt Orford was a tremendous individual player,' Cronk said. 'He's got the brilliance, but I see our team as having even more skill out wide and I want them to get the chance to use their ability. That doesn't deteriorate from my football game. I played in the halves through my time at Brisbane Norths and filled in for Scotty Hill when he was injured last year, so it's not new territory for me. But it's a big challenge.'

Cronk would become elemental in the Storm's resurgence.

The pre-season started well with a trial win against Parramatta. The Melbourne club were also keen to reinvigorate flagging interest at their games. It was felt the main members of the crowd at Storm games were ex-Kiwis and ex-Northerners and they desperately wanted to broaden their supporter base.

Storm boss Brian Waldron was behind the campaign hoping to reignite local interest. He claimed the Storm had the second biggest following in the NRL with 554,000 supporters, but many questioned if these were real supporters or just Melburnians who had 'heard' of the Storm.

The TV ads were based on the slogan 'You can't avoid rugby league this season'.

Waldron wanted to target the Melbourne audience.

'Victoria is a unique environment for rugby league and as such, a distinctive approach is needed to promote the game in this market,' Waldron said. 'The new Melbourne Storm advertisements are fun, exciting and edgy. We believe the use of humour will bring a new awareness to the game as humour cuts across all demographics.'

The TV ads were followed up by newspaper and radio advertising. The Storm also started a development program for juniors in Victoria. The program would help uncover one of its future stars, Gareth Widdop.

The Storm hoped to build on the fact Origin was returning to Melbourne for the final game of the series. The stage was set for Billy to shine. After all, he was one of the best known faces in league—one of its most marketable players.

Billy was attracting big time sponsors. One of his greatest fans was Tony Devers, a loyal Storm supporter (eventually made a life member) who was general manager of Suzuki Australia. Devers was one of the first business people to back the Storm when Ribot was knocking on doors to get sponsors. Essendon had rejected Devers for a sponsorship, so when Ribot came knocking he had no hesitation in signing up with the Storm. Devers would become soldered to them—even through the salary cap crisis when some sponsors walked away. Over the years Devers developed a belief in the culture of the team and not even the salary cap rorts wavered his view. He could always see the sun past the shadows. And time proved him right. Part of the excitement and allure for Devers was the brilliance of Billy. Devers was impressed by Slater's confidence, his pursuit of the best. Over time he saw him grow from a young man unsure on his feet to a team leader and one of league's elites. He had no trouble putting the Suzuki name next to Slater.

He first met Billy when he arrived in Melbourne in 2003. 'He was humble and clearly had a degree of confidence,' Devers said.

Cameron Smith had just arrived as well. Devers remembers: 'Ribot declared "we've got a couple of good ones here". They were boys playing in a man's team against big men when they first arrived. To their credit they got through it.'

Suzuki was a sleeve sponsor with the Storm from the start. Billy became an ambassador for Suzuki. Devers said market research showed people responded to him. He had a boy-next-door look and was down-to-earth.

'He was someone who came from nothing to being a supreme athlete. He has no problems and he is already thinking of life after football, owning a horse farm and helping people with disabilities to ride. With Billy, all his intentions are good.'

Nicole had the same down-to-earth manner as Billy, Devers said.

Nicole and Billy were part of an annual Suzuki fun day. Billy joined in the 'hot lap' contest where Storm players try to beat each other's time at a raceway on Melbourne's outskirts driving Suzuki sports cars.

Billy loves cars and has a Suzuki Kizashi sport AWD. He also owns a classic EH Holden with black dice as valve caps.

The relationship with Billy and Suzuki continued, and he later asked Nicole to co-star with him in a Suzuki commercial.

Billy appeared in many Suzuki ads over the years. In a raunchy ad in 2010, Billy picks up a brunette in a Grand

Vitara and heads to the beach with his surfboard on the top as the background track playing 'you can have it, if you want it'. His mates Dallas Johnson and Cameron Smith are also in the commercial.

Billy's profile took off rapidly and he became one of the most bankable stars in the NRL, earning almost $1 million a year from his league salary and sponsorships. He promotes everything from bananas to potato chips, sports drinks, children's books and he has also featured on a stamp as an Aussie legend.

(Billy was also sponsored by Adidas and travelled to Spain to shoot a commercial, the country his great-grandfather had left so many years before. He was marketing a new Adidas boot with Carlton AFL player Dale Thomas.)

Research by Melbourne-based sports consultancy Gemba on the asset power of athletes found that Billy was clearly at the top of the list for players in the NRL. He also ranked in the Top 20 when 1500 respondents were asked to cite who had the best drawing power among both international and national sports stars. He was seen as 'dedicated, inspiring, fair and competitive', according to Gemba. That popularity continued through his career. Gemba said Billy was 'one of the most adored athletes across Australia'.

The Storm were also later to beat the bad publicity of the salary cap crisis. A survey after the explosive revelations in 2010 found the Storm were still the most liked club in the NRL because they were seen as 'successful', 'inspirational', 'on the way up', 'popular' and 'exciting'. (The Storm were also ranked as the most deceitful club in the wake of the salary cap rorts.)

Devers stuck with Billy as he stuck with the Storm. But would Billy always stick with the Storm? Devers was also an Essendon supporter and could see why at times Billy was attracting interest from various AFL teams. He was good under the high ball, speedy and fast thinking.

Lance said there was some interest in Billy from AFL teams but nothing firm was put on the table. 'There was talk about it, but I don't know if there was anything firm [an offer],' said Lance. The Storm did a lot of cross-training with teams such as North Melbourne and Carlton. Lance felt the AFL players were learning more from the Storm than the other way round. 'We were teaching them more than they were teaching us, basically we were showing them how to tackle, we had a lot of defensive sessions with them. '

North Melbourne chief Donald McDonald was instrumental in building the relationship with the Storm. 'I think our boys learnt AFL is a hard game and a tough game,' Lance said.

The relationship with the Kangaroos started in the 2005 pre-season and North Melbourne actually employed Storm to help them to provide tackling and wrestling training.

Donald McDonald, then assistant coach, had done the same training at Hawthorn. Kangaroos coach Dean Laidley said: 'Donald did it at Hawthorn ... and he just thought it really helped in those last five or six games and ... we thought it appropriate for this group'.

Collingwood also used the Storm in their training.

'Going into the season it won't be on a weekly basis but it will be fortnightly,' Laidley said. It wasn't just a muck around run, it was a serious plank of the AFL club's training platform.

McDonald said the Storm helped the Kangaroos' tackling techniques in the pre-season sessions. It was a contra arrangement meant to benefit both clubs.

'The Storm taught us tackling techniques like putting the shoulder in, pushing through with their legs in a tackle,' McDonald said. 'What was important was that we just had a different voice telling us what we could do.' The Storm's new assistant coach Michael McGuire and Lance were keen to continue the sessions.

But the big Storm forwards were found out when they had an open mock–Aussie rules game and quickly petered out in the fast-flowing football on a big field. 'I think they would have preferred the field a bit tighter,' joked McDonald.

Billy and Cameron Smith only had a few cross-training sessions because they were normally given extended leave over the Christmas period when the teams got together. McDonald said Billy had all the ground skills, including the ability to pick the ball up at speed, to be a top AFL player, but any move from one sport to another was a gamble.

'If you don't grow up playing a sport it is very difficult to change codes,' he said.

McDonald admired Billy's courage under the high ball.

The Storm kept up affiliations with other AFL teams and sometimes Bellamy sat in the coaches' box during AFL matches when he had the chance.

Devers believes Billy's training with AFL players helped make him one of the 'best high-ball defensive players in the league'.

At one stage Carlton coach David Parkin expressed his view that Billy was a prime AFL target. The Storm also played a mock game against Carlton.

'He [Billy] can run, jump, kick off both feet, he is certainly an elite athlete,' Parkin said after the match.

League writer Roy Masters said 'AFL coaches have told me Slater would be an instant hit in their code. They have seen him leap high above the pack to gather the ball, like a superhero catching a falling baby. But they also know he has hands as big as old baseball gloves, and can gather a ball on the ground at speed. He seems to go even faster when his body is tilted away from would-be tacklers, and slices between opponents with body angles that would make a chiropractor grimace.'

The Storm, though, would do anything not to lose Billy. But first they would have to negotiate Billy's terrible year of suspensions. His actions would disappoint his teammates and his clean image on the field would take a big hit. The year 2006 would be Billy's *annus horribilis*.

Storm won the first two games of the season and Cronk was assuming his role at halfback with aplomb. Bellamy still referred to him as a 'kid'. But two subsequent losses meant that by the fourth round the Storm were struggling in tenth place. There was little indication they would rise to become minor premiers and grand finalists. And when they lost their star player for almost three months it seemed a lost cause.

Billy had always had a bit of niggle in his play. But his action in kicking the head of Tigers player John Skandalis was seen as an ugly slur on his reputation. Billy explained it all away as an accident. He was trying to struggle free to pass the ball and Skandalis had hold of his ankle. He struck out with his other foot and just didn't realise Skandalis's head was there.

He was charged with one of the highest grade dangerous charges in the league: a grade five kicking charge—only just under the radar of the most severe charge, which might have produced a far lengthier suspension.

He was put on report for the kick during the 2 April game at Leichhardt Oval, which the Tigers won 30–28. Billy scored 2 tries in the match. Billy was trying to pass the ball with Skandalis holding on to his ankle and appeared to be angry because he was being impeded. In the same motion Billy lashed out with his leg, which glanced Skandalis's head. After the incident Skandalis chased after Billy, which caused some laughs and uproar amongst the Balmain followers on the hill, who started shouting some derogatory chants at Billy. Dave Kidwell (who would later become a Tigers stalwart) tried to hold Skandalis back as he went after Billy. After the final whistle, Billy went up to Skandalis to apologise.

Skandalis said he had accepted Slater's apology. 'It's all over and finished,' Skandalis said. 'He apologised after the game on the field and I accepted it. I hope nothing more comes of it. I don't want him suspended. It happened in the heat of the moment. I don't mind leaving things like that on the field. It just stunned me.' Asked about the crowd reaction, Skandalis said: 'They must have seen it. They stuck with me which was good. We got away with the win. That's enough for me.'

But Billy wouldn't get away with it. He was cited to appear before the NRL judiciary three days later to face a serious kicking charge.

NRL prosecutor Peter Kite told the hearing that if Skandalis was injured: 'If he had have been, it is my respectful submission that this would be an ungraded charge and a more serious charge'.

Billy entered a guilty plea and only contested the grading. He admitted to recklessly striking Skandalis with his boot. But Billy claimed it was an accident. 'I do realise it was clumsy and careless and I realise I've done something wrong,' Slater said. 'But in no way was it intentional.'

Storm football manager Dean Lance (Lance had moved on from his assistant coaching position) claimed the Tigers players were told to slow down the Storm players and Billy was reacting to the niggling tactics.

Storm chief executive Brian Waldron said the contact with Skandalis's head was 'slight'. 'There was no injury, no blood and he received no treatment,' Waldron said. 'Slater said he had wanted to break free of Skandalis so he could back up the player to whom he had off-loaded.'

Kite said it was:

> ... conduct both unfair and grossly excessive. Whether or not you knew it was John Skandalis, you knew it was a Tigers player. When you looked down to see what was going on, did you see his head? It was pretty hard to

miss. You resented being restrained by the player on the ground and you reacted by kicking out at him.

This was a deliberate and forceful kick to the head of a player on the ground. When one looks for mitigating circumstances, there are none, nor any provocation—nothing to justify kicking an opponent on the ground, let alone in the head. The offence was one of the highest at the graded level.

The judiciary concurred and gave Billy a seven-match ban.

As well as missing Origin—even if he was selected—Billy was out of the game until round 13 when Melbourne were due to play the Sydney Roosters.

'It's very disappointing, I've got a fair while on the sideline now,' Billy said. 'I've got to cop that on the chin and get back to playing football after that. Our case was that it wasn't intentional, I apologised straight away. It was one of those things where I didn't mean to do it.'

It looked like all hopes of rejoining the Maroon Origin team were over. 'Yeah. It looks like it, doesn't it? That's up to them [selectors],' Billy told the press.

Billy was forced to sit back and cool his heels as the Storm suddenly ran into red-hot form. They won their next five games with Inglis taking over from Billy at fullback. After defeating the Eels in June, they took top spot and didn't relinquish the position for the rest of the season, taking the minor premiership.

Billy's part in the Storm's big year was undermined by a further string of offences. His return in round 13 proved disastrous. Not only wasn't he selected at fullback, he was on the interchange bench, and when he ran on to the ground with just twenty-five minutes to play, he was put on the wing and was almost immediately back in trouble. He was accused of using a dangerous throw, or spear tackle, on Rooster Ryan Cross.

Billy didn't address the subsequent judicial hearing, which decided to suspend him for two matches.

Storm football manager Dean Lance said: 'I thought it was disappointing — I thought we put up a very good case and had a very good argument. There's no complaint from this end, Billy will do his two weeks, and [then get] back to business.'

But Bellamy had other ideas. He was deeply disappointed with his young charge. Not only would Billy serve the two weeks but Bellamy would put his return on hold for another two weeks. He decided the best way to prepare Billy for a return to first-grade was to get him to play with the Storm's feeder clubs—Norths Devils in Brisbane and the North Sydney Bears in Sydney.

So there was Billy, feted as an Origin star, forced to suddenly backtrack to where he started. Was it punishment or truly a way of bringing him back to his peak?

Looking back on what he had achieved and what he became, it was a joke. During Billy's time at the North Sydney Bears one of his fellow players asked for his autograph. It was embarrassing for someone rated already as one of the game's best fullbacks, its best rookie only two years earlier and having scored one of Origin's greatest tries. There was Billy running around in a sub-standard New South Wales premier league. Mentally, it could have damaged any great player on the crest of a wave. But not Billy.

Bellamy tried to justify his decision.

'It's not a decision that we took lightly, but Billy's played twenty-five minutes in ten weeks,' he said. 'We were quite prepared, after his seven weeks suspension, to play him because we thought he could manage playing first-grade. But he's had another three weeks off since then basically and we just think it's too much footy to miss to be at his best.'

Bellamy was trying to protect the roll the Storm had established. Remarkably, Billy wasn't part of it. 'Obviously the other reason is the team's going well so there aren't too many reasons to change our team.' he said. This was a no-nonsense approach by Bellamy, threatening to isolate the very star players the Storm needed. It was a high-risk strategy.

The decision really wiped Billy from any chance of playing in the Origin series.

'That's Mal's [Meninga's] problem and the selectors' decision up there,' said Bellamy. 'My decision is to put on the best team for the Melbourne Storm on Friday night, and that's where it stops and that's where it starts.'

Although New South Wales had won the first Origin game of 2006, Queensland fought back to win the next two games and take out the series and win back the Origin trophy. Billy's Storm teammate Cameron Smith played a huge part in the victory, the last in Melbourne where Billy could only be a spectator. These were hard yards for a competitor such as Billy to sit through, also having to watch from the sidelines in Melbourne.

Annus Horribilis

The world seemed like a very dark place at this time for Billy.

Billy didn't return until 7 July in a game against the Broncos. It was part of a mid-season eleven-match winning streak by the Storm.

It was a powerful return and a testament to his strength of character.

Billy set up the opening try of the match and played a vital role in another one. A last ditch tackle on Bronco Brent Tate ensured a 10–4 victory. Everyone hailed it as an impressive return and it augured well for the play-offs as the Storm powered ahead at the top of the ladder.

But then Billy's year went pear-shaped again on 5 August. He was charged with striking Tigers player Shannon McDonnell on the head with his forearm during the Storm's 46–4 win. He was hit with a striking charge and then another two-match suspension, which the club didn't contest.

His surfing mate and former captain Robbie Kearns was upset that his mate Billy was in the bad books again. Kearns declared:

> He [Slater] has let himself down and he has let his team down.
>
> It's been a very disruptive year for him in the sense that he has missed seven games for the kick and missed another two games for the spear tackle, so I bet you he is going to look back on this year and think what a bum year. But at the end of the day, he's a great player. He knows he's done the wrong thing.

Billy was amassing a lot of carry-over points in the judiciary with his charges. The club decided it was best not to appeal so he wouldn't get further carry-over points.

Lance said: 'The club is disappointed but there's not much we can do about it. He works very hard to get the intensity up in his game and I'd be disappointed if he did anything other than that.'

It was hard yards for an enthusiastic Billy who just wanted to get on with the business of playing at elite level. It looked like his whole year could be a waste. But there was a carrot at the end. It seemed almost inevitable the hot form Storm would make the grand final. Billy would get his chance to win an NRL trophy (now known as the Provan-Summons trophy) to add to the team's JJ Giltinan Shield as minor premiers.

Billy said a few years later looking back on the string of suspensions that he wished it had never happened:

> I'd probably like to wipe it away from my memory.
>
> I ended up getting suspended three times. It's the only time I've ever been suspended in my whole career, and it hit me head-on. It hit me hard. It was frustrating and a bit embarrassing, but all you can do is try to move on.
>
> I don't think it was what you would call part of my game, but it just kept happening. Three suspensions from three games, more or less—I just had to get back into playing football.
>
> I sat out for about seven weeks to start with and I was on the bench in my next game back. I only got a run with about twenty minutes to go against the Roosters

and I ended up putting Ryan Cross past the horizontal. I was just trying to get into the game because I'd been out for so long. I was just being over-eager, I think.

Billy said he hoped he would become a better player and a better person.

Meanwhile, the Storm were raging on to a grand final berth. Billy returned on 26 August just in time to play the last two games of the regular season and get himself into some form for the finals. The Storm were pumped. They won the minor premiership convincingly by eight points and all the new young breed were firing.

Former Storm forward Dennis Scott predicted a strong finals performance by the young brigade. 'I think it is a real advantage that the young guys … are not tainted by any brush, as far as past lack of success,' Scott said. 'They're going in enthusiastic. I know that all the young kids are absolutely jumping out of their skin and this is a great opportunity for them to play semifinal football.'

Storm recruitment manager Peter O'Sullivan told *The Age* that the team had a core group of players aged in their early twenties, including Smith, King, Crocker and Billy, who would carry Melbourne forward for many years to come.

'Our senior players, even though they are around twenty-two, twenty-three, [have] all played upwards of seventy NRL games and I think that's when you hit your peak, between seventy to 180 games. So our players, even though they're young, they are at the peak of their performance,' O'Sullivan said.

The stage was set for Billy to resurrect his year and he didn't let down those who had shown faith in him. Everyone seemed to be having their two cents worth about what was wrong with Billy's game.

Former Test player Mark Geyer, brother of Billy's Storm mate, Matt, said it appeared Billy's timing was off and he needed to step up to keep his position in the team for the finals campaign. 'Basically, I think Billy has to have a big game against the Eels to cement his spot in the side coming into the finals,' Geyer said.

Queensland legend Wally Lewis also was concerned Billy was getting careless in his tackling. 'He's got to be a little bit careful. His arms have been sneaking up a little bit high again and his biggest danger is once again suspension,' Lewis predicted.

But Billy did stand up and it was his defence that helped save the game for the Storm. Billy made a try-saving tackle on Parramatta centre Brett Delaney, who looked like he was racing away to score. Somehow Billy ran him down and pushed him over the sideline, with the Storm holding on to win 12–6 to get the Storm into the preliminary final for the first time since 1999.

The Storm then defeated St George 24–10 to book a place in the grand final. But the victory came at a terrible cost to Billy's surfing mate Michael Crocker, who suffered a potentially career-ending knee injury. During a tackle his hamstring was effectively pulled off the bone at the knee. He faced months in a leg brace after surgery and wouldn't be able to play or train until early in 2007.

Billy had a quiet game and some reckoned he should be replaced at fullback by Inglis. Blues coach Ricky Stuart was among the critics. Bellamy stood firm and said Billy would stay in the number one jumper.

Billy had slipped all over the Telstra Stadium surface. He sent out an urgent SOS to his sponsor for new boots. He was wearing long studs and found he couldn't get a hold on the greasy surface. Adidas sent Billy a couple of new boots with shorter studs to trial for the grand final.

Bellamy said he wouldn't be without Inglis or Slater for the grand final. 'Both those guys are special players, and they have to be in the team. They are game-breakers who are capable of doing things others can't. We'd love Greg to get a bit more ball as well, but defensively he is very important for us in the centres. He scored a great try on the weekend, but also saved one.'

Slater knew he had to lift his game to thwart the experienced Broncos.

The Broncos had not been in a grand final since 2000 but they had played many more finals than the Storm. (Brisbane had an impressive record—five grand final appearances for five wins.) The Storm went into the grand final as favourites after their dominating season. The grand final set up an interesting contest off the field—the master Wayne Bennett trying to undo his understudy Bellamy. (If there was a masterstroke by Bennett it might have come earlier in the year when he gave his players a week off during the middle of the season—an almost unheard of action in league. Some of the Broncos even managed a quick trip to Thailand. It was designed to help relieve the pressure on the team after they collapsed in the previous two finals campaigns and after their heavy Origin duties. Lockyer later credited it for giving his team time to refocus.)

At the grand final breakfast Bellamy revealed, tongue-in-cheek, the two coaches didn't have that much in common. Bellamy told *The Sydney Morning Herald*'s Roy Masters: 'There's been no big blue or anything,' he said. 'Apart from football we haven't that much in common. He's got his farm. I like the beach. He doesn't drink. I like a beer.'

Cameron Smith was given the honour of leading out the Storm after a fantastic season. Bellamy had changed the captain throughout the year between Geyer, Kidwell, Hill and Smith. But for this big one, Smith was in charge—the Dally M Award winner for 2006.

Channel Nine's 'Rabbits' Warren reckoned Melbourne would have the balance of power from the Sydney crowd at Telstra Stadium. Billy took the first hit of the game, confidently catching a high ball from the kick-off. He was involved in the first points of the game but not the way he wanted. Videos showed he'd been unfairly penalised for a strip. The Broncos Shaun Berrigan tried to burrow through near the Storm line but Billy came away with the ball. Referee Paul Simpkins penalised him. Replays showed that the ball had just fallen into Billy's arms after Berrigan lost control of the ball. Lockyer kicked the penalty to get the Broncos on the board.

A bit of Scott Hill magic produced the first try for Steve Turner and the Storm in the corner. Hill was on edge. He had to sit out the 1999 grand final victory and wanted to end his career at the Storm on the highest possible note before he headed off to play in the English Super League. Hodges replied for Brisbane with a try after a spectacular Brisbane backline movement. Broncos prop Shane Webcke was playing out of his skin in his last game for his club. After 254 games in the league, he was also desperate to add another premiership to his curriculum vitae.

Early in the second half Matt King replied with a try for the Storm. Brett Tate then scored in the corner as a desperate Billy tried to roll him into the corner post. There was only a few inches in it. Gould backed Brisbane to ride out the last ten minutes with the score 14–8. 'They [Brisbane] know how to win the tight ones,' Gould said. Lockyer then made a great left foot strike to score a field goal and force Melbourne to score twice to win the grand final. The final score stayed at 15–8. After the final whistle, a number of Storm players were inconsolable. Ryan Hoffman let all his emotions out as he contemplated the defeat, Hill was distressed as well. Webcke fell into the arms of Bennett, and dedicated the win to him. Broncos' hooker Shaun Berrigan took out the Clive Churchill Medal. Billy and his teammates sat disconsolately on the ground watching as the Broncos colours were blown in a ticker-tape shower over the celebrating Brisbane team.

Everything for Billy was thrown up in the air late in the year when there was a family tragedy. Both Nicole and he flew back to the Far North to be with family. He was excused from pre-season training. It was a terrible year.

CHAPTER EIGHT

GLORY DAYS

Melbourne had stamped its authority on the competition and showed it was a force to be reckoned with for years to come. The older clubs had enjoyed a run of halcyon days at some time in their history, but Melbourne—still seen as the baby-faced boys of the NRL—was starting its first golden era.

While the Storm could glory in its rising stars, one player suddenly struck like a meteorite out of nowhere. Out of the ruck of aspiring players stepped a seventeen-year-old who had the gall to think he could match it with league's best. Israel Folau arrived in the same pipeline as Billy, Smith and Cronk—from the ranks of the Norths Devils feeder club. He'd created a big impression as an Australian schoolboy representative and had shocked everyone with his maturity, playing as a sixteen-year-old in the hard Queensland Cup competition. But could he realistically be thought of as centre in a team that had just won a minor premiership and were hot off a grand final?

Born in western Sydney from Tongan parents, Folau grew up learning his football at Goodna on the edge of Ipswich, near Brisbane. He was just a suburban boy, but now the strong-legged kid was becoming king of the city. (Goodna even named a street after him by the time he was twenty-one. That was an honour for Folau, but an unintended problem for the local council as scavengers often stole the sign because of Folau's fame.) Folau was the Storm's new season strike weapon.

Billy could only stand back in awe as the young, confident player entered the realm of league's tough men. If he could handle the rough and tumble of the Queensland comp, the talent squad at the Storm (including Peter O'Sullivan who'd scouted him when he was fifteen) were confident he would handle the NRL. He was on a contract worth just $35,000. But would he stand up to the intense training of a first-grade side and the week to week hammering and travelling they went through?

Folau didn't take long to show his mettle. In his first game of the year at Olympic Park in Melbourne, the Storm were struggling and looking nothing like premiership favourites against an average Tigers outfit. Bellamy blasted his team at half-time and they came chastened from the dressing room ready to right the ship for Bellamy. The Storm clawed their way back against the Tigers and then in the opening stanza Folau showed why everyone was so excited about him. Smith put up a high bomb and leaping like a gazelle, Folau snatched the ball from his Tiger combatant and fell to score the match-winning try. Melbourne had scraped in 18–16 and saved themselves a full-time blast from Bellamy.

The headlines the next day showed what an impression he'd made in his debut first-grade game: 'New Storm boy off to a Flyer'; 'Storm teen proves he's years ahead' and 'Folau proves hard act to follow'. Folau scored 2 tries in the next game against Canberra.

By the end of March, there was talk Folau might even don a Maroons jumper. Both Billy and Smith said it was too soon for such a giant leap.

Billy said: 'I'm not sure. He's only a young kid and he's only played two first-grade games. I'm sure he wouldn't be thinking about playing Origin and I'm sure if you mentioned it to the coach [Bellamy] he'd laugh at you. He's definitely a talented kid. He's physically mature and he's built well. It's pretty frightening. But I think he's got a fair bit to go with his learning, how he can improve.'

Smith said: 'He's a wonderful athlete. He's big and he's strong. But he's only played two games. It's a bit hard for him to take that next step and play Origin. It's a big jump—I think I played fifteen or sixteen games when I went up, and it was difficult. It's more intense and it's a lot harder mentally.'

Both declared he was a certainty for selection in years to come.

Bellamy suddenly had an embarrassment of riches at his hands. Not even seasoned winger Steve Turner, one of the two try-scorers in the 2006 grand final for the Storm, could get back into the team. The Storm fought tooth and nail to stop Turner from leaving the club during the off-season. Turner was also coming back from an ankle injury. But a fully fit Turner wasn't straight back into the Storm line-up. A young upstart was keeping him out!

Bellamy said Billy was playing as well as ever and he wasn't dropping Geyer, Inglis or Folau either. Turner had to cool his heels for a few more games. 'I'm not going to leave someone out who deserves to stay there,' Bellamy declared.

By April the Storm were angry that Channel Nine were not giving them coverage in their home state despite being premiership contenders again. The club felt the programmers were treating them with disdain.

'I'm very disappointed with the treatment we get. It's disgraceful,' Waldron told the *Herald Sun*. 'It's a major concern, the lack of exposure for us on free-to-air. It isn't as if we're not an attractive proposition. We figured very well in the ratings for our game against Wests Tigers.'

Channel Nine promised the coverage would swing the Storm's way as the season progressed and the Storm built up their finals campaign.

As happened in most years, April was the time people started nominating who should be in the Origin line-ups. Again, Billy's name was pushed forward for fullback but many doubted he could unseat Karmichael Hunt. Billy had had a top start to the season, scoring 5 tries and playing a hand in 9 others by round 7. His upper body strength was growing and he had dropped the untidy parts of his repertoire. (Folau had scored 7 tries in the same period and was well on his way to breaking Billy's record of 19 tries in a debut season—he'd score twenty-one).

Queensland Origin stalwart, winger Willie Carne, believed Billy should get the nod over Hunt for number one jersey for the Maroons. 'I'm a big fan of Karmichael Hunt but I wouldn't be playing him, I'd be playing Billy Slater in the fullback position,' Carne said. 'I reckon they're a better side with him there and I'd put Karmichael on the bench. I think Billy Slater this year is playing a little bit better footy. Karmichael's playing good footy, but he's not beating anybody, he's just running into everyone ... it's a funny one, it's going to be a tough battle.'

But Billy missed out again—not that he could have played anyway.

Maroons coach Mal Meninga believed he had to dish out just a bit more tough love to Billy. He wanted to stay loyal to the Queensland players who had clinched the Origin series in 2006. Billy understood the logic.

Billy expressed his feelings after the announcement of the Queensland team: 'It might have been a different story if they hadn't have won it last year but they showed a little bit of loyalty to the players ... and that's fair enough,' Slater said.

As Melbourne lamented its lack of exposure on Channel Nine, it put in another blockbuster performance out of prime time. Played late on a Saturday afternoon in Sydney, the match was a prelude to the grand final for the next two years.

Manly's home ground of Brookvale was a hoodoo space for the Storm. Something always went crazy or wrong at the ground and it proved a Storm graveyard more times than not. The hoodoo didn't end when Billy ran out with the Storm on 26 May. The Storm had only won there once in six games in its history, and then only by a lucky point. Leading up to the match the Storm had been on a roll and had only lost one match in ten games in 2007. They were sitting second on the ladder. The game had an interesting match-up between Billy and his Manly opposite Brett Stewart, a rival for the Test jersey. Billy once denied he even knew who Stewart was when asked about him at a press conference. They had an intense rivalry.

The bitter struggle ensued for eighty minutes and was only decided by a field goal—by none other than ex-Storm hero Matt Orford—to give Manly a one-point win, 13–12. But in the melee of players throwing themselves at each other, Billy smashed his cheekbone in two places when he accidentally ran into his teammate Samoan Sam Tagataese, who had just come off the bench. He would need two metal plates inserted into his cheek to fix it. Manly's George Rose also broke his fibula. Both he and Slater were stretchered off and the Brookvale curse continued. (Four years later the curse would continue with crazy on-field and sideline fights between the two teams and two send-offs and then an amazing moment when Billy helped save Manly's David 'Wolfman' Williams from a severe spinal injury when Williams fell to the ground in agony after fracturing a C6 vertebrae. Billy cradled him and sought quick medical attention).

Billy was out for at least six games and now had no chance of making it back for Origin 2007. He had to set his sights on the grand final 2007. In the meantime, due to his injury, he was eating a lot of pumpkin soup at home.

After the Manly loss, the Storm would only lose one game during the rest of the season. Folau was carving up the competition and breaking records all around him. Inglis was well on his way to earning an Australian jumper after just two seasons in the game. Billy could only look on as they excelled, and then had to watch as Queensland took out another Origin series. He really wanted to be back in maroon to share the sensation of giving it to the Blues.

Meanwhile, cracks started to appear in the Storm's facade. In July, chief executive Waldron complained that stricter controls on the salary cap meant they could lose star player Matt Geyer. Recruitment manager Peter O'Sullivan said the NRL's stricter policing of match payments in 2007 would make it difficult to offer players new deals. Players on incentive deals were pushing the Storm unexpectedly over budget. Accountants were called in to try to sort out the mess. Keeping Geyer seemed like a lost cause. He was the last surviving member of the 1999 grand final squad and the club's most prolific try-scorer.

'He's an institution at the club, and we want him to play if he wants to play,' O'Sullivan said. Whether we can afford him is another matter.' He complained the league was losing players to the English Super League and to the French rugby who could afford to pay big money. The club, after negotiations, were able to keep Geyer for another year.

With Israel Folau's football value growing by the minute, the Storm faced a big dilemma on how to keep some of the league's biggest stars in its ranks without breaking the salary cap. Waldron had told everyone on the Storm board that the club would do everything in its power to keep the big four—Smith, Cronk, Slater and Inglis.

Billy agreed to terms on a three-year extension to his contract. The deal would take him to the end of the 2010 season. Slater said, 'This is my fifth year and they've been great to me through some tough times, especially last year I didn't have the best year and the Storm stood by me through that tough time,' Slater said after the announcement.

It was believed his contract was worth over $400,000 a year.

There were signs Waldron was not always dealing face to face with his colleagues and upsetting old links. Norths Devils' chief Mark Murray was in shock when he was told that Waldron was going around Brisbane's rugby league clubs looking for another feeder club. Murray of course had contacts throughout league and there was nothing too private he was going to miss in the Queensland mix.

Murray decided to approach Waldron directly about it. For him such a move seemed insane—of course Norths had supplied all the current Storm stars. It was a proverbial goldmine of talent with no end in sight. Waldron was purely seeing it as a business arrangement. There seemed to be no sentiment to the arrangement that had worked so well. Waldron was apparently in talks with Brisbane club Easts Tigers.

A lot of the biffo came down to money. Waldron didn't want to pay for things such as flights for Norths' players coming to trial or play in Melbourne and vice versa. Obviously the club was trying to pinch money wherever it could to keep its stars.

Murray said:

> He made life pretty difficult for us up here. Brian didn't want to invest in the development program and what was going on up here. His idea was that everyone had to pay their way. We had to pay for airfares for Melbourne players coming back here. Everything seemed angled as to what was to his benefit.
>
> Clearly this wasn't going to work and he was selling himself to other clubs around Brisbane. Just going in and asking people if they would take over from us, without talking to us first.
>
> I said to him 'What was going on?' and he denied it and I said 'that is what these other clubs are saying you are doing'. We agreed that if he was going to do that again he would tell Norths first.
>
> Then a month or so later one of my contacts from a rival club rang and said 'Your mate's at it again.'

An upset Murray went straight to the Broncos and set up a new feeder club arrangement with them to start in 2008, ending a nine-year association with the Storm, and leaving Waldron out in the cold. It was a bitter blow and left the Storm floundering for years trying to find a feeder club of equal strength. Storm founder Ribot would have been livid. (Ribot left the Storm in 2004, handing full ownership to

News Limited. News Limited later appointed former St Kilda boss Waldron as the new chief executive.)

Behind the scenes the Storm was trying to shift money from one year to the next to stay under the salary cap. In the process, they had to ask the senior players to take a pay cut, which would be repaid the following year in 2008, saving the club about $100,000. There was tension everywhere in the club as the financial honchos tried to find a way to keep its talented squad happy.

Paul Kennedy revealed in his book, *Storm Cloud*, the depth of the feelings in the Storm management as the football department fought with the administrative department. In an email sent by recruitment manager Peter O'Sullivan to the Storm financial officer Cameron Vale, O'Sullivan blasted Vale for, in his words, letting the side down with what he saw as petty financial requirements. The Storm had used a system whereby players were able to use redeemed points from credit cards to turn into vouchers to pay for household items. It was one of the benefits in keeping players happy at the club. Vale had sought official approval from the NRL for the scheme and requested it not be included as a salary cap item, but this was rejected by the NRL's salary cap auditor Ian Schubert.

An upset O'Sullivan complained Vale had let the cat out of the bag as the team were on the cusp of a great era after 'years of hard work' and just missing going down the gurgler in the early 2000s. He was angry Vale had gone to the NRL to seek ratification. He didn't believe it needed official sanction.

'I am at a loss to why we are self-destructing,' O'Sullivan wrote. 'I fight a daily battle with Craig [Bellamy] on players' income and loosing [sic] players because of our success but I am losing the drive to try and hold this squad together ... I implore you to help me with small things that may help a player.'

From the players point of view the season seemed to be steaming along and they were on cue to redeem last year's grand final loss. A lot of the financial dealing and bids by the club to keep managers happy were happening without their knowledge. Most of the players never asked each other how much they earned. It just wasn't what they did. But the salary issue was a ticking bomb ready to explode.

After surgery, Billy was back for the match against the Rabbitohs on 7 July. He then scored 2 tries in the whitewash of Newcastle in the next game. The Storm were firmly planted at the top of the ladder and Billy was making his comeback to plan.

Smith lauded the new feel-good Bellamy who was taking more of an interest in what the players had to say, including the leadership group consisting of Smith, Johnson, Geyer, Cronk and Crocker. Bellamy even asked for their advice before pursuing a new player, Clint Newton, midway during the year. He'd gone from Bellyache to a version of Dr Feelgood, and the squad thrived on the new approach.

'It wasn't until last year that we had a say in what we did at training and the way the team trained. Before that, it was sort of his way or the highway,' Smith told *The Sydney Morning Herald*'s Brad Walter. 'But he's really learnt in the last few years that if he works with his players he's going to get the best results out of them and he's done really well as a coach.' Bellamy was almost a lay-down misère to be named NRL coach of the year.

Most credited Bellamy for the growth of his players. He was an integral part of their game.

In the latter part of the season the Storm recorded big wins against Newcastle and Canberra, but only scraped home against Cronulla in round 21 in early August. They thumped the Bulldogs and the Titans in the last two games of the season. They were minor premiers again, this time by six points.

While pundits talked endlessly about Billy's abilities before the finals (Billy ranked as one of the ten most talked about people in Australia after Prime Minister John Howard in the week leading up to the grand final), his greatest admirers were always his family—all with a great knowledge of football.

His dad Ronnie knew all about Billy's speed and endurance. When he was younger, Ronnie used to drive his ute behind Billy as he ran along the Far North roads as part of his fitness work. If things went pear-shaped in Melbourne or he wanted a break, Billy was quick-smart back to home at Garradunga (the Slaters had moved there from Goondi Bend). It was a raw and friendly place with all the feel of the Far North wilderness. Billy loved coming home, putting his feet up and helping clean out his dad's bar fridge with his mates. One of Ronnie's constant activities was to nab a dolls eye (brown tree snake) that slipped into their back patio area. Garradunga, out in the cane fields, was full of snakes. Once, a taipan slithered past the barmaid at the Garradunga pub straight into the store room, just as if it was going home.

Ronnie spent much of his time, apart from watching the races, watching replays of Billy's games and he was pleased with his son's progress.

Billy had always been a reactive player and this had been instilled in him by Ronnie. He wasn't one of those players who studied endless videos of the opposition before a game. 'I always told him, footballers don't think, they react,' Ronnie said. 'Billy has phenomenal speed and anticipation and that's what his game is built around: speed, reflexes and reactions.'

His father's cousin Sue Astorquia, a stalwart of the Innisfail league and a pillar of the *Innisfail Advocate* newspaper, reckons Billy had invented a new way of playing. And when she sees him, he reminds her totally of Ronnie, or Mophead:

> When Billy first started playing NRL, he reminded me so much of his dad Ronnie at that age that I would yell out 'go Mop ... go Ronnie'.
>
> He makes it look so easy. He has the same expressions and style as Ronnie when he is running, Ronnie was very agile around the scrums. He could sidestep with either foot, dodge or weave, and had the ability to see an opportunity before it actually was there.
>
> Ronnie and Billy are masters at reading the game and can anticipate what is going to happen and they

position themselves to be at the right place at the right time to grab any opportunity that could come along.

Sue admires Billy's physicality and how he uses it to bullock players out of the way or save tries with some great feat of agility.

Now when I watch Billy it's his own style. He is so quick off the mark and can sidestep with either foot and weave and change direction at speed. He doesn't wait for the ball to come to him and uses his body between the opposition player and the try line to save a try. He is a try-saver in many ways, jumping high for the ball, all this leads to him having control of the ball. These are all new aspects that he has brought into the game and I see more players using them now. Billy was the first to introduce them and execute these moves so successfully. He is a natural and has charisma. Above all he is a winner and very competitive.

Billy has brought a new level to the fullback position and is more involved in the attacking play than most spectators realise. He will leave his fullback position unguarded and come in to make up the extra man, he comes up to the forwards like a lock forward. By doing this he is the extra man in the attacking line to have an undefended extra player (his opposition fullback is still back behind the play defending his own position), this creates the one man over gap for a try scorer to get clear of the defence. By the fourth tackle, Billy is back in

> the fullback position to defend his position. This means he is covering a lot of extra ground, he is always back in position when they kick the ball. It can be risky play. What he has developed, he's created a bigger workload than a fullback normally has ever had, as it involves double the running to be back in position.

The Slaters and Nicole were there as much as they could be to watch Billy's games. Nicole had become great friends with Cameron Smith's partner Barb and other partners from the Storm line-up. The partners and wives often went to the movies together outside football.

Everyone was talking about the star Storm backline. They dubbed it the '$2 million backline', one of the best of the modern era.

The Storm disposed of Brisbane in the qualifying final 40–0. It was massive turnaround from the previous year's grand final and there was no Shane Webcke hero. The Brisbane players who had allegedly goaded the Storm players about their grand final win during the year had to eat humble pie.

The publicity might have got to the Storm a bit as they had a struggle to shake off Parramatta in the preliminary final.

Bellamy was worried Storm were over-pumped after a nervous win over the Eels, 26–10. He blamed himself.

'At the starts in each half, we weren't on our game. At the start of the game, I thought it might have been because we didn't play last week, but the start of the second half was really poor actually. To the guys' credit, they hung in there and ground away,' Bellamy said.

He may have pumped them up too much. 'Perhaps I put too much time into the emotional side of it. We started off with plenty of effort and plenty of desire, but perhaps we weren't as effective as we could have been and I take the blame for that,' Bellamy said. 'We probably just got a little bit too pumped up.'

Billy had injured his medial ligament in his right knee in the game. He bravely said he'd take a needle to help get through the pain for the grand final. Experts said it was a dangerous move. Roosters doctor John Orchard said the risk of aggravating a medial ligament injury was so high that even if it was for a State of Origin game, he wouldn't think of it.

He warned there was a high chance of further damage, which would rule Billy out of Test calculations—the Test team to be named days after the grand final.

'For a grand final, it's a no-brainer,' Orchard told *The Sydney Morning Herald*. 'But this is the only game of the year you would do it. It's not the sort of injury you would normally needle because of the risk of injuring it further. You wouldn't even do it for a State of Origin game because of the risk of being out for club games afterwards.'

With 81,392 people packed into Telstra Stadium it was no surprise that the Manly team started ferociously and the first target was Billy. Jamie Lyon and Glenn Stewart raced in to throw Billy headlong into the turf and were put on report. The game had only been going a minute. The old Storm–Manly enmity was coming out.

Billy didn't flinch and had a memorable first half, cutting swathes through Manly and racking up 127 metres in the first forty minutes. Inglis showed his strength in the twenty-fourth minute with his first try, running over the top of Anthony Watmough and through Matt Orford. Storm led 10–4 at half-time and there was no indication yet the Storm were about to run riot. Inglis went to a new level as did winger Anthony Quinn. Inglis's second try was a crowd pleaser. In the fifty-sixth minute, following a bust by prop Brett White, he took the ball 60 metres from the try line, sprinted around Michael Robertson and, fending him off, raced in to score.

'Inglis answered criticism of his move to five-eighth this season by scoring 2 tries and throwing the final pass for 2 others, while Smith was heavily involved as usual at dummy half and Slater electrifying at fullback,' Walter wrote in *The Sydney Morning Herald*.

Billy was involved in one ugly incident shortly after half-time. Brett Stewart rose high to catch a ball when he was hammered by Crocker and Slater. The Manly-biased crowd booed as there was no penalty. Stewart was left disorientated and had to be helped from the field and took no further part of the game. Two hours later he still had no idea what had happened to him.

'I've got a headache, I can't really remember much,' Stewart said. 'I remember just being out there in the first half, but not much of what actually happened, and I remember half-time, but that's it. I can't remember the tackle. A few people have told me what happened, but I've got no idea.'

Billy finished with ten runs for 157 metres, offloading twice, making two line breaks and four tackle breaks.

The Storm ran away with the game and made it a one-act affair, winning 34–8. Inglis was named the Clive Churchill Medal winner as the best on the ground.

Billy declared: 'That was a ripper. It was a tough game in the first half, but we toughed it out and in the second half we just let it rip.'

Manly were angry their fullback had been taken out and believed it had cost them their momentum. Stewart later just shrugged it off as one of those things a fullback can expect under a high ball.

Melbourne were singing the Prince song 'Purple Rain' at the end of the match.

More honours were to flow. A few days after the grand final, Cameron Smith was named in the Australian team as captain to play New Zealand. Cronk, Hoffman, Inglis and Crocker also won Kangaroo jumpers. (The Storm's international reps numbered seven as Jeremy Smith and Jeff Lima were both selected for New Zealand.) Brett Stewart, though, had beaten Billy for the fullback position.

Bellamy said Billy was unlucky.

'It's out of his control. All he can control is how he plays and he played wonderfully, he's had a wonderful year and he was great again [Sunday] night, so it's up to the selectors and at the end of the day if he keeps knocking on the door they'll let him in at some stage,' Bellamy said.

'I don't want to get into an argument or whatever. All I'm saying is I reckon he's played well enough to get in there. It's hard to argue against Stewart. He's had a really good year and he's played State of Origin. It's hard to argue with that.

Billy's been a little unlucky, but there'd be other players in the same boat.'

In a late surprise, Justin Hodges injured himself before the Test and young Folau was jettisoned into the team—he had not even represented his state yet. He was part of the team that hammered New Zealand 58–0, scoring a try and becoming the youngest player ever to represent Australia at eighteen years and 194 days (the previous youngest was Billy's Innisfail compatriot Kerry Boustead at eighteen years and 310 days).

Despite missing out on an Australian jumper, Billy had come up with a grand final medal and could finally have something to show for his efforts: his first major trophy. The Storm had lived up to their potential. Some said if they'd lost the grand final—two in a row—they would have disintegrated. The fact the Storm stood up for the count showed they were made of harder stuff.

In 2008, Billy would finally get the plaudits he deserved, in fact, they would keep flooding in. He'd win an Australian Test jumper, join in an Origin series win, be named the best rugby league footballer in the world and, to cap it all off, become a father.

CHAPTER NINE

LAPPING IT UP

Billy and Nicole had settled beautifully into the inner city lifestyle of Melbourne—busy hanging out at coffee bars and enjoying the relaxed atmosphere of Richmond. They pursued their own careers just a stone's throw away from each other—Billy had his football down at Olympic Park and Nicole her art in her Richmond studio. And the surfing beaches weren't too far away for Billy. They'd befriended the Storm's number one ticket holder, pop guru Molly Meldrum, who lived in the suburb. Everything was cosy and they'd often take their dog, Puggles, for a walk about town.

Molly, the announcer from ABC's legendary TV show *Countdown* who had helped put so many Aussie bands on the map, was helping put the Storm on the radar in Melbourne with his enthusiasm. He was so in love with the Storm he had the team's logo tattooed on his bicep. Molly divided his loyalties between his beloved St Kilda (the Saints) and the Storm and loved both codes. As the Storm rose and rose it was a win-win situation for Molly. He could trumpet his tribalism in Melbourne for the Saints, and if they weren't doing so well, trumpet the Storm, who were nearly always in finals contention. Molly and Nicole would chat at Storm matches and later Nicole would do some paintings for him, including a portrait of his favourite dog Ziggy. Molly put the portrait in his lounge room and adored it.

Molly explained his love of both AFL and NRL. 'I love going between the two,' he said, referring to his two football allegiances. 'They're both thoroughly entertaining in their own right.'

Molly always held a post-season party for the Storm players at his house. Once the police were called because it got too noisy—there were allegations of a thrown bottle—but mostly it was just a jovial affair for players and wives and partners, surrounded by Molly's Egyptian relics.

* * *

Billy started 2008 with a bang, scoring 3 tries in the Storm's victory over the Warriors.

By round 9, the Storm were on top of the table again and on their way to their third consecutive minor premiership. Billy's form made him an irresistible prospect for state and international honours.

Bellamy was ecstatic at Billy's start to the year and said he was an obvious choice for Australian fullback. Everyone noted that Billy had erased many of the errors from his game.

He was entering a comfort zone with the other players, not always looking for that solo flash of brilliance, being more of a team member. Bellamy said he wouldn't have anyone else but Billy at fullback.

Bellamy said:

> To me, it's a real big rap because I mean it. That's not being disrespectful to the other fullbacks, but I would not swap Billy Slater for any of them. The thing is, I just enjoy watching him play. Even if he was on the other side, I'd enjoy watching him play. You don't need me to tell you how good he's been playing. He's probably been our best player this season.

Brad Walter wrote in *The Sydney Morning Herald* at the end of April:

> Storm fullback Billy Slater needs only to survive tonight's match against North Queensland to win his first Australian jersey when the team to play New Zealand in the Centenary Test is named tomorrow. Slater, who is one of the form players of the premiership ... is understood to have made such a compelling case for selection in the opening six rounds that only injury or suspension will stop him from making his international debut in the 9 May Test at the SCG.

Australian coach Ricky Stuart was suddenly in the Billy camp and enthused about his prospects. They'd even set up bookmakers' odds for the fullback Test position. But Billy's rival Brett Stewart, the incumbent, was favourite at $2.10.

Former Test fullback Garry Jack couldn't split the pair. 'Slater's in the best form of his career. He's just fantastic.' Jack said. 'But Brett Stewart is back to his best and is the Test incumbent. I dead-set can't split them.'

Stuart said Billy's form had put great pressure on Stewart and Hunt. 'A player like Billy Slater hasn't played for Australia but he is placing enormous pressure on the others,' Stuart said. 'I'm sure the selectors are enjoying what Slater is doing. I'm also sure Karmichael Hunt and Brett Stewart are up for the challenge.'

Slater believed he'd also hit peak form.

'I think I am as mature as I've been over the past five years,' Slater said. 'I'm always trying to add new things to my game and improve my skills. I suppose I am getting better each year so you could probably say I am in my best form.'

Stewart admitted Billy had been cutting up the competition.

When the prestigious position for the Centenary Test against New Zealand was announced, Billy's name was at number one. It was a huge achievement and an honour in league's big celebratory year. He couldn't have timed his run into top form any better.

Before 34,000 people at the SCG, Billy ran onto the field with many of his Storm teammates including Smith as captain (he'd replaced Lockyer who was injured). It was another Storm player, Inglis, who provided the inspirational moment when he scooped the ball back from it going into touch to set up Gasnier for a try. The Kangaroos led the match 22–0 at half time and went on to win the game 28–12.

League legend and commentator Peter Sterling reckoned Billy should have been man of the match (Smith was man of the match).

'While Australian selectors opted for Cameron Smith as man of the match in Friday's Test, I felt that the new Aussie fullback was best on ground with a series of superb try-saving tackles,' Sterling wrote in the *Newcastle Herald*.

Billy was now obviously back in the hunt for an Origin jersey. But he was facing an uphill battle. Queensland selectors always stuck with incumbents who had won the previous Origin game. That meant Karmichael Hunt was in the driver's seat for Origin.

His Storm mate Smith did his best to get Billy into the fullback role for the Maroons telling the press Billy was playing the best football of his career.

Smith gave a very honest and thorough description of his mate:

> He was pretty shattered when he got dropped [from Origin]. I guess it played on his mind a little bit in 2006 and last year, where he was probably trying to do too much to get back into the rep scene. With a couple of injuries and suspension that kept him out, he struggled there but he's worked really hard over the last eighteen months. He's got a bit of a cooler head, where before he used to try for the big plays and win matches off his own

> bat. He's been playing really well and he's been the best fullback in the comp.

Billy defied tradition and was named at fullback. Hunt was selected at five-eighth. He said he now valued the Maroon jersey more than ever after his stint away.

'I think I've earned it a little bit more now. I'd only been playing for eighteen months in first-grade when I was picked last time.' Slater said losing the jersey was tough. 'It's a passion of mine to play for Queensland and to get dropped hurt me a little bit. It's been three years since I've played Origin football, so hopefully I've learned a lot out of that and I can take those lessons into this game.'

The series had added spice for all the Storm players—those playing for the Blues and those playing for the Maroons. Bellamy was the new New South Wales coach. He had the inside knowledge on almost all the players on both sides! Bellamy admitted later he hated the prospect of coaching against the players he held in the highest esteem such as Billy, Smith and Cronk. Would he really send in the Blues storm troopers to attack Billy like the previous Origin coaches? Not only that, but his rival was Mal Meninga, one of his great mates from the Raiders era. It all seemed a bit too personal, with long held and trusted links at risk. Despite his sometimes ferocious reputation, Bellamy was actually very close to his players and treated them with respect. Origin would be a hard learning curve for him. He'd discover he was a better club coach than a representative coach. Origin was a hard test for players, and just as much a tough and a cut-throat business for coaches. Bellamy would find it the toughest role in his life.

Billy had his chance to make up for the lost Origin years as he ran onto ANZ Stadium in Sydney on 21 May as Queensland's fullback. The New South Wales fans had turned up in droves after the NRL warned it may take an Origin game away from Sydney and give a game back to Brisbane or Melbourne. But 67,000 people answered the call. Billy was expecting the usual onslaught from the Blues. The Blues went on forays up the middle and through the ruck, rather than opting for the high ball and putting Billy under pressure. Billy had one of the first plays that almost led to a try in a length of the field movement. The Blues had more intensity and quickly were able to nullify Queensland's attacking stars.

Bellamy had settled his troops in well during the week. It was a tough call for him, blooding so many inexperienced Origin players. The Blues were littered with debutantes including his own Storm winger Anthony Quinn. They all passed the test though. Quinn ended up scoring 2 tries while his Storm teammates playing for Queensland were shut out of the game. New South Wales ran out 18–10 winners and Bellamy was on a high and looked like he had cemented his place in Origin coaching ranks. Billy had just a run-of-the mill game and was in danger of being put on the bench for the next game.

Tough Blues forward Willie Mason said Bellamy had the right to be considered his own coach—no longer an understudy. He'd made everyone play to their strengths.

'He's moulded himself into one of these coaches where he's a motivator, a mentor, a friend. He's his own coach now and has a lot of respect. He's got the right game plan for us and we stuck to it,' Mason said.

But there was trouble brewing and it was coming out of Bellamy's own house at the Storm. He'd upset his mate Cameron Smith by employing the Storm's wrestling coach, John Donehue, to help with the Blues tactics for game one. For Smith, complaining about someone using wrestling coaching, was like the pot calling the kettle black. Smith reckoned the Blues smothering tactics had made the first game a farce and uninteresting.

'I'd like a faster game but … it's probably not going to happen, so we'll just have to adapt to the way Craig is going to get his team to play,' Smith said. 'At least we now know what we're up against and we know what their goal is in defence.'

Smith said coaches like Donehue should be confined to club coaching. The issue of wrestling would come back to haunt Smith, who later in the season would fall foul of the authorities for an alleged grapple tackle—something Donehue had taught him.

Storm winger Steve Turner was called up for New South Wales for game two, making both Origin sides awash with Storm talent. Never had one club, apart from the Broncos, been so dominant in Origin ranks. The Storm had Smith, Billy, Crocker, Inglis, Folau and Johnson in the Maroons, while the four Storm players for the Blues were Brett White, Quinn, Hoffman and Turner. There weren't many people left running the Storm back in Melbourne! It was huge testament to the Storm and a huge testament to Bellamy. He was training players so well he was in danger of losing momentum in the club's premiership run because of the representative duties. The relentless style of football in Origin always took its toll on players. There were fears the Storm might not survive the torrid end to the season as they sought to secure consecutive premierships.

Both Origin sides were rocked by late-minute changes after Hayne was ruled out for the Blues with a suspension and Queensland lost Hodges due to a suspension.

Billy was put on the bench for game two and Hunt went back to fullback. Some pundits saw it as Billy being sacked. But it turned out to be a masterstroke by Meninga: he reshuffled his team into a new strike force and brought in Scott Prince at halfback and moved Thurston to five-eighth. He could use Billy as his strike weapon. Billy didn't have to wait long to be deployed.

As the Maroons ran riot in front of their home crowd at Suncorp, the Blues had no answer. Debutante Darius Boyd scored 2 tries almost in identical circumstances after barnstorming runs by Inglis. Inglis fended off Gasnier—one of the best centres in the game—like he was a little fly in the course of setting up the first try. Queensland raced away to a 16–0 half-time lead. The Queensland forwards paved the way for the star-studded Maroons backline to shine. Inglis was unstoppable. Billy, wearing the unfamiliar number fourteen jumper, was having a strong game as well. Queensland ran away to win 30–0 in one of the most comprehensive wins in Origin history. Billy got to celebrate amongst his family and in front of 52,000 fans—mostly jubilant Queensland supporters. It set up another great Origin decider.

The Storm players were doing it at both ends. Their season was still on track and they would only lose two of their last eight games of the regular season to make it three minor premierships in a row.

Everyone was on edge for the Origin decider. In front of 78,000 fans at ANZ Stadium, Billy was again on the bench. But this time he would get to make a decisive mark on the match and on the Origin series. It was a case of Storm versus Storm for the first 2 tries as the upstart Folau waltzed over Anthony Quinn to score twice in two high-flying acts. Commentators asked if Folau was actually wearing a Superman cloak such were his aerobatics. Folau was everywhere and made 116 metres in thirteen runs. The game was a torrid, hard match with several brawls. Both sides refused to relent. Crocker was accidentally knocked out by the football after a Blues kick and he fell to the ground semi-conscious. The game was locked at 10–10 until some Jonathon Thurston wizardry broke the deadlock in the sixty-seventh minute. Thurston burst through the Blues line and ran down field. Who else was there in support but Billy? He raced away to score near the uprights in what turned out to be the winning try for Queensland. Billy finally had his moment of justice. He'd scored the winning try in an Origin game and helped secure an Origin series victory for Queensland. It was what he had dreamt of all those years ago and now it had come true. He was over the moon.

After the match an exhausted Billy told ABC's *Grandstand*:

> I was just stoked to get over. That's the toughest game of football I've ever been involved in. At 10-10 all, it didn't look like anyone was going to break until a bit of Jonathon Thurston magic, so the way we hung in there in the end there, we were on our line the whole time, that was just a great Queensland effort, I think. Mate, toughest game I've been involved in. It was just unbelievable, they threw everything at us, I just think this bunch of blokes, we've got something special here.

Before his famous try, Billy said he and Thurston actually had a little chip and chase organised on the right and then suddenly he saw Thurston go around to the left so 'I just followed him'. It was a great day for Billy, but a worrying end for Bellamy who seemed so confident at the start of the series. Now there was talk he might walk away from the Origin job. But fellow coach Brian Smith said it might have been more of a case of the players not being up to the coach, rather than the other way around.

During the finals campaign of the 2008 NRL season, Bellamy cost his club $50,000 after he and chief executive Brian Waldron were fined for comments questioning how and why his star captain had been charged over a grapple tackle.

The Storm raced through to the finals and Billy would score 14 tries for the season. All seemed well as the Storm tide ran on but they lost their qualifying final and had to fight back to regain momentum. But then the team hit a brick wall. In a bitter battle with Brisbane in the semifinal—which they won to deliver Broncos long-time coach Bennett a sad farewell with a bit of Inglis magic in the last minute—Smith was sensationally put on report for an alleged grapple tackle on Sam Thaiday.

Cameron Smith appeared to have his arm around Thaiday's chin as fellow Storm player Jeremy Smith locked up the Bronco player's arm. Thaiday and Smith were of course Queensland teammates and Smith insisted there was no malice in the tackle. Because of carry-over points from a charge earlier in the year, Smith faced at least two games on the sidelines if he was cited, and then found guilty.

Cameron Smith pleaded his innocence saying he didn't twist or choke Thaiday. 'I don't think there was any intent involved,' he said.

The review committee cited Cameron Smith. Smith faced a grade one charge of unnecessary contact with the head or neck. A fired up Bellamy told *The Age* the charge was unfair and so was the charge against Jeremy Smith. The press got stuck into the Storm, accusing them of using the chicken wing tackle. A furore broke out in league circles and the Storm's image was slurred.

Talking about how Jeremy Smith held Thaiday's arm in the controversial tackle, Bellamy said 'He's got hold of his arm. He hasn't bent his arm, has he? The position he started in, it stayed in,' Bellamy said. 'What do they want him to get hold of? Get hold of his head? Get hold of his balls? It … pisses me off, mate,' he told Stathi Paxinos.

Bellamy would never let go of the fire over Cameron Smith's charging. Would it cost the Storm a premiership? Smith was cited and then the judiciary found him guilty of the charge and suspended him for two matches, ending his finals campaign. It was a big blow. Jeremy Smith was given one week for his part in the tackle.

After the suspension Bellamy attacked the media for the publicity given to Cameron Smith's tackle and said many of them had pre-judged Smith. Bellamy believed Smith was 'hung out to dry'. Bookmakers had had Smith at $1.18 to be found guilty and $4.25 to escape the charge, Bellamy claimed. Bellamy went on:

> The press conference after one of the best games we've seen in a long time or the most tough contest with a finish like that, the press conference got hijacked by some of you guys in the media that had him hung out to dry straight away, and then it continued for four or five days. I know it's not all of you, but there are some sections of the media that seem to have an agenda against Melbourne and certainly on the grapple tackle.

The Storm played Cronulla in the semifinal and a spat ensued between Australian and Cronulla coach Ricky Stuart and Melbourne chief Waldron. Stuart said Smith deserved the charge. Stuart said the charge was clear: Smith had hold of Thaiday's head, 'not knee'. Stuart called Waldron 'a flip' after Waldron hit out at him for commenting on the case before the penalty was announced.

There were brickbats being thrown around everywhere. Members of the judiciary called on the Storm to apologise to them over what they perceived were allegations on the judicial process. But when the Storm did apologise—not acknowledging they had questioned the judicial process—after the grand final, one committee member said the apology was 'half-arsed' and too late.

Smith's suspension was something that would always sit hard with Bellamy. In his book, *Home Truths*, he wrote 'to have the wrong thing done by him, that was hard to see.' Bellamy said Smith had been a great ambassador for the game. 'I did not like what happened to Cameron Smith when he was suspended. Cameron was wronged and I believe that to this day.'

The Storm defeated Cronulla and made it into the grand final to face Manly once again. The Storm had taken a beating in the judiciary and on the field. Manly's players were firing—Manly's halfback Matt Orford was racing away to win the Dally M Award for best and fairest player of 2008.

Smith called it the hardest day of his life as he sat in the stands at the grand final and saw his Storm team torn apart by Manly. Manly's kicking game destroyed the Storm. Billy couldn't run, Folau couldn't fly and Cronk couldn't kick. It was hard to believe such an elite group of players could be so totally outplayed. It seemed to start all right for Billy. Channel Nine's 'Rabbits' Warren noted when Billy flew high to take the ball in the opening minutes 'he hasn't been that high since he rode a 17-hand horse for Gai Waterhouse in track work'.

But Billy wouldn't reach the great heights that he had achieved during the year. Brett Stewart revelled in sticking it to Billy in the walkover. There had hardly been a more comprehensive defeat in a grand final, 40–0. Everyone was rocked back on their seats. It was only 8–0 to Manly at half-time, but the second half saw a torrent of Manly class. Eagles' winger Michael Robertson scored 3 tries and then to cap a grand day for Manly, the club stalwart Steve Menzies, in his final game, scored in the last few minutes. The Storm offered little resistance. There were no excuses. Billy was eaten up by the Manly defenders wherever he turned. They kicked to his weak side and stopped him running right and mangled his flair when he tried anything brave. With no Cameron Smith, the lynchpin, the Storm were rudderless.

Rugby league writer Brad Walter has watched Smith at close hand for most of his career. Naturally, as a dummy half, he has a high possession rate in almost every match he plays. But almost everything the Storm do comes out of Smith's genius. And he is also a great tactical kicker—a rarity for that position. Smith's nickname is the architect, not just because he helps design Storm play—but because he has the lean physique of the stereotypical architect.

Walter said:

> Smith is Melbourne's control man. He's controlling things from dummy half, he's the one who decides if they are going to pass or kick. Very few players have been as dominant. He takes the ball almost every tackle and decides where the play is to go. He's just much smarter

than many other players. Because he sometimes kicks from that position [from dummy half] he gives his team an added boost, one because he's further upfield when he kicks, than say if he's passed to the halfback, and secondly he also puts all his players onside. He creates the time and space and Cronk absolutely feeds off him.

Once he's gone, they lose all of that. I'm pretty sure the record of the Storm when playing without Smith is very poor.

Despite the grand final defeat, it was not a miserable year for the Storm. Accolades and representative jumpers kept flowing for the players. For Billy, after the grand final misery, it was actually his *annus mirabilis*.

He'd assumed some seniority in the team with Bellamy and earned his respect. He'd become a fine football student and was helping educate the Storm backline. Bellamy had given him that leeway, even though he thought Billy too often thought outside the square.

* * *

The first accolade that flowed in Billy's amazing spring and summer of 2008 was his selection in the Australian World Cup squad. Billy had the chance to star at home at an international level.

But it turned out a bittersweet campaign. Australia stormed through the World Cup and Billy led the way. The Kangaroos scored 180 points and conceded just sixteen in casting aside New Zealand, England, PNG and Fiji to make the final. They started as red-hot favourites against the Kiwis to win the World Cup at Suncorp Stadium in Brisbane on 22 November.

Billy would be voted the best player in the tournament but a blunder in the final soured the great accolade. Billy couldn't understand it. If he did something amazing he was a hero, but if one of his edgy plays didn't come off, he was a villain. It was like his Origin try in 2004, when he created a sensation, a defining moment, about which the press liked to harp on about. So when he made the big mistake, they harped on about that as well. The pain and the glory.

The World Cup produced an unlikely set of combatants. The Brisbane and Australian stalwart Wayne Bennett was working as a coaching co-ordinator for the Kiwis. Was it a ploy to help make the World Cup more competitive by sharing the Australian talent? If the gamble was to work, was it worth Australia actually suffering the incredible embarrassment of losing the final? It seemed the Bennett know-how was the only way the Aussies were going to get beaten after such a convincing performance in the tournament.

In the final before a sell-out crowd at Suncorp Stadium in Brisbane, Australia looked like they had the Kiwis well in hand, leading 16–12 at half-time. But soon after the break the Kiwis hit back with a try. Many said the turning point was when Billy, with nineteen minutes to go in the final, was being pushed towards the sideline, just out from the Australian line, when he 'recklessly' threw the ball back infield only for it to land in the hands of Kiwi Benji

Marshall. Marshall ran away for a try. Some said it changed the momentum of the game. But the critics often forgot there were other blunders by the Australian players in the game that may have proved costly, including a two-pointer given away by Joel Monaghan. While Australia replied with a try by Inglis, the Kangaroos couldn't recover with New Zealand running out winners in a shock 34–20 result. Coach Ricky Stuart and his team stood disconsolately in the middle of the field before the presentation.

In the heat of the loss, Stuart made some wild allegations against the referee and the ARL—that the match had somehow been concocted to give New Zealand a victory to pump up the World Cup brand. Most of the focus, though, was on Billy's wild pass.

The fallout ran all the way up to the Far North. Even Billy's mum was asked by one newspaper about the infamous pass:

> I made a pledge to myself that I wasn't going to read what the media said about him.
>
> At the end of the day they are out to sell newspapers and don't care about the feelings of the people they write about or their families. Because that did touch a lot of my family. It was very hurtful.
>
> Even Billy made the comment 'gees, they [media] jump ship pretty quickly'.
>
> One day he was a hero and the next he was a villain. I thought that was very, very harsh considering there are sixteen other players in the team. Billy will make those

mistakes. He is going to try anything. When it comes off it is spectacular, when it doesn't it looks very bad. But we have moved on.

Billy refused to shoulder the full load for the World Cup final defeat.

He said he'd taken on Kiwi winger Manu Vatuvei before during the football season and it had worked.

'In round one this year, I did get past him in exactly the same position on the field,' Billy told *The Sydney Morning Herald*.

'It's just the way I play. If I see an opportunity, I'm going to have a crack at it more times than not. If I had my time over again, I'd do something different. We lost the game, they scored a try. I'd be stupid if I said I wouldn't do it differently. I saw an opportunity, I went for it.'

Billy seemed to resent the focus the media suddenly put on him for the World Cup loss:

> You guys [the media] have done a fair job. But I don't think ... I wouldn't put it all on my shoulders. You make mistakes out on a footy field. Mine resulted in a try. I'm sure there were other mistakes out there. That's the way the cookie crumbles.
>
> I had a great time, a great five weeks in camp. It's something I'll never forget, even though we didn't get the result. To play for my country was something special. That's rugby league. You take the good with the bad.

Billy's relationship with the media was always a bit chilled.

He left the World Cup tournament with a big missile from tournament commissioner Greg McCallum. He said any more of Billy's feet-first attempts at tackling would not be tolerated and he would face a striking charge and a long suspension if he attempted it again. McCallum was commenting on Billy's try-saving sliding tackle against Kiwi Jerome Ropati. Billy had also attempted the same intercept against Manly's Michael Robertson in the NRL grand final.

'If he cuts a player open, nothing will save him,' McCallum said. 'It's got to stop. It's a dangerous practice. The only reason he wasn't charged was because he made no contact with the player, but this was centimetres from a catastrophe.' Playing on the edge was always part of Billy's game.

Billy had little time to relax before he received one of football's biggest honours.

He was voted the best footballer in the world. The Golden Boot Award was started in 1985 by a British rugby magazine. Billy was presented with the Golden Boot statuette at a Rugby League Players' Association dinner in Sydney, where he also took out the RLPA's representative player of the year award. Slater beat eight nominees for the Boot including Greg Inglis, Johnathan Thurston, Benji Marshall and England's Tony Peacock. A panel of twelve rugby league writers and former internationals, including Wally Lewis (the inaugural winner of the award) and Peter Sterling, cast votes for league's highest honour.

Billy was unlucky not to also pick up the other major

rugby league award of the year, the Dally M Medal. He missed out on it by the narrowest of margins to Matt Orford and it was only because of a suspension after he gave a flurry of upper cuts to Dragons winger Jason Nightingale's head in round 19 that caused him to lose points after a suspension. Billy was only a point adrift of Orford. Under the Dally M rules, players lose three points for every week's suspension incurred.

Slater found some solace from the grandson of league legend Dally Messenger (after whom the awards are named). Dally Messenger III said he was always in awe of Billy's skills. 'I don't believe in the supernatural but when I first saw Billy Slater I said, "My God, the old man's reincarnated,"' Messenger said.

Billy said he was humbled by Messenger's comments.

'When you hear the grandson of Dally Messenger, the bloke who basically started rugby league in Australia, saying that I'd reminded him of his grandfather, it's a huge honour,' he said.

Billy Slater was also named the Storm's player of the year—the first time he'd taken out that honour. The awards kept flooding in.

One of his most treasured awards came from his home town of Innisfail. The Cassowary Council decided to rename the major sports ground in Innisfail, Callendar Park, after Billy. It was now the Billy Slater Oval. Billy was left speechless by the honour. The field meant so much to him. It was where his father and grandfather had played and where his football had all begun.

Councillor Ian Rule said Slater deserved the honour. He said Billy winning the Golden Boot was akin to Makybe Diva's three Melbourne Cups.

The greatest thrill, though, for Billy in the midst of all the hype, honours and controversy was the birth of his first child, Tyla Rose. Billy left the World Cup to be by Nicole's side for the birth.

'Seeing what she went through … mums are far tougher than footy players, that is for certain,' Billy said. 'Thankfully she looks a lot like her mum,' he quipped to *The Sun-Herald*'s Danny Weidler.

While Billy was hoping to spend a lot more time at home with the new baby, an unlikely offer came along that saw him leave for a week to sunny Queensland. Billy was offered a role in a new TV series, *Australia's Greatest Athlete*, and he took the challenge on with both hands.

Billy was up against some famous foes, including A-league soccer player Joel Griffiths, Olympic gold medallist pole vaulter Steve Hooker, rugby international Lote Tuqiri, AFL star Brett Deledio, cricketer Andrew Symonds, racing car driver Jamie Whincup and Ironman Ky Hurst.

Hurst and Billy became great mates. They shared a common past—both were born at Nambour Hospital. And of course, they both loved the surf. 'My mum told me we were both delivered by the same doctor, I believe a Dr Dick,' Hurst said. There must have been something dynamic in the Nambour water in the 1980s to produce such two outstanding athletes. Hurst held seven ironman titles, was an Australian champion long distance swimmer and had twenty-eight Australian surf titles. He was one of the favourites for the title.

The show's film crew bunkered down for a week for the shoot at Couran Cove on Stradbroke Island, just north of the Gold Coast. It was a jovial atmosphere but there was no mistaking the feeling of competitiveness amongst such elite sports people.

'It was completely professional, all the athletes were there to win,' Hurst said. 'Everyone was competitive in what they did and Billy was no exception to that.'

'Billy and I got on really well and we have spoken regularly ever since that show. Billy is one of those athletes who would be good at whatever they chose to do.'

Billy excelled in almost every event. But when he and Hurst were to face off in the beach sprint obviously everyone thought Hurst would scream it in.

'He absolutely dished me,' said Hurst of Billy's performance. Billy ran second to Steve Hooker but still distanced Hurst.

Hurst found out when he was about to exert his dominance on the event, the courses were changed or altered. The endurance swimming event was just three minutes, while Hurst normally swam over twenty minutes, and when Hurst thought he would cream it in the surf ski event, Lote Tuqiri complained he might drown, and the event was held in a pool.

The competitors then paddled on duckboards so none of them would tip into the water. But whatever the event, Billy was shining and up on the podium more often than not.

In the first event, Billy came second in the golf challenge, then second in the basketball challenge, before winning the one-on-one try-challenge, rock climbing and high ball challenge. He blitzed the field with 1385 points and was named Australia's Greatest Athlete for 2009 (the series was screened the next year). He backed it up in 2010 by winning it again—this time only just from ironman Shannon Eckstein.

Hurst found Billy a funny guy whose best attribute was that he was 'just down to earth'.

'I had a really good time doing the show. Billy was very level-headed and didn't get carried away with his success.'

It was an amazing year and Billy felt on top of the world.

CHAPTER TEN

YOU KNOW WHO

The Storm squad was sore and wounded as the 2009 season got underway. Billy was among a host of Storm players still getting over the rigours of the World Cup campaign. The Storm also lost the precocious talent of Folau to the Broncos.

Pre-season training was thrown into disarray and Bellamy lamented how the disruptive start to the year was making life difficult for last year's grand finalists.

'We had six players come back from the World Cup who didn't start training until January,' Bellamy said. 'We had about another nine players that had operations this year and there's probably five or six of them that didn't start until after January. Most of our core side from last year were either at the World Cup or having operations, so they didn't really have a good pre-season.'

Bellamy didn't reveal the team's woes until later in the

year. In the interim he just put on a brave face hoping the ship would right itself.

His team started poorly and was struggling in eighth place on the ladder. By May they'd only won half their games. And they weren't winning by the huge margins that they were used to. The departure of Folau had thrown the Storm backline into disarray. The centre pairings weren't working. That all changed with the arrival of Brett Finch from the Eels in late April. When Finch took over the five-eighth role, the Storm started to find its rhythm. Inglis moved back to the centres. Finch, a former Blues player, was fitting well into the star-studded line-up and was also forging new friendships amongst a sea of Maroons. Finch and Billy would become great mates.

Finch enjoyed his new role. 'I'm probably just there to give Coop [Cronk] a hand, he's the dominant ball player and I'll just fit in and work around him,' Finch said.

When Finch later worked on *The Footy Show* with Channel Nine he interviewed Billy before his 250th club game and told viewers what he thought of him—even though Finch was one of the deflated Blues players' Billy ran straight past to score his amazing 2004 Origin try. 'I am great mates with you, I know how down to earth you are, how important your family is, you've stayed grounded as much as you possibly can, but you will go down as one of the best fullbacks, if not *the* best fullback, this game has ever seen.'

A humbled Billy replied: 'It's very humbling to be honest. I'm just a kid from North Queensland that loves his footy. Footy has taught me respect and selflessness.'

As Origin time approached there was the perennial debate on whether Billy would get the nod for the fullback role for the Maroons or if he would come off the bench to replace Hunt, while Hunt took the pressure in the first stanza.

Former Blues fullback Garry Jack said the choice was a no-brainer:

> I think [Hunt] is probably going to end up being closer to the ruck rather than at fullback ... Karmichael Hunt has done nothing wrong, don't get me wrong, he hasn't had a bad game, but the other bloke is just exceptional.
>
> I think they're just playing ducks and drakes with selection so that NSW has to try and guess which way they are going to go. He [Slater] is the current Golden Boot winner and he is in outstanding form and he just brings a lot more to the team, not only individually but with his brilliance, than Karmichael Hunt—and Karmichael Hunt is a very good player. There's not too many blokes who can bring what Billy Slater can bring to the team, that's why I think he should start and he probably will start.

He scoffed at claims Hunt's body was heftier and better suited than Billy's to withstand an early Blues onslaught:

> That's ridiculous ... he might be bigger and there's no doubt that he's a very good player but I don't think he brings as much to the game as what Billy Slater does. Billy Slater plays against big blokes every week and fires

and performs at the highest level so I don't think there's much credence in that because he [Hunt] has got a bigger body he can absorb more punishment.

Billy was now stronger and wiser. He'd hit 90 kg, his biggest weight since playing, and he was tackling harder than ever. There was no way he would miss running on the field for the first Origin game in his adopted home of Melbourne. For the first time in Origin, the first game of the series was to be played in Melbourne, this time at Etihad Stadium. The Maroons would enjoy strong support.

The Blues were trying to head off a fourth consecutive Origin series loss. Bellamy was also trying to save his Origin coaching position. It all seemed to start well for New South Wales when Hayne ran down the sideline, seemingly to score, but then only for the try to be reviewed and denied—the video referee finding he'd touched the sideline by the barest possible margin. Queensland hit back and in the next major play, Billy went steaming through the Blues defence to touch down a Smith kick only a millimetre from the dead ball line. The try was awarded and the Maroons were up and away. Sport was sometimes cruel: just a millimetre between pain and glory.

Billy was showing guts and determination in his tackling. He smashed Hayne in a try-saving tackle and forced him to lose the ball and then he smashed forward Luke O'Donnell who was powering over the line to score, only to see Billy's momentum force him to also cough up the pill. Billy was the first person to jump on and congratulate Inglis after

Inglis scored a sensational try down the sideline to start the Maroons second half. Thurston was landing goals from everywhere. The Melbourne crowd were getting a Storm-led party to remember.

The Blues came back into the game with 2 tries and then a kick through from Lyon was picked up brilliantly by, as 'Rabbits' Warren pronounced, 'you know who'—Billy. The Maroons ran away winners 28–18 and the Queensland juggernaut rolled on.

A stomach virus swept through the Maroons camp prior to the second Origin game and Billy was among the long sick list. One player was so bad he was hooked up to a saline drip. But it couldn't stop Queensland, even after a fractured jaw forced Inglis off the field early on, the Maroons' attack stayed strong, making it four Origin series wins in a row with a 24–14 victory at ANZ Stadium on 24 June. (NSW won the dead rubber on 15 July.)

The Storm held on tenaciously to fourth spot from June. Billy was again in superlative form and leading the try scoring table for his club. He'd bag eighteen for the season. The Storm had turned their poor start around and were on a high going into the finals after two resounding victories against the Roosters and the Warriors.

Roy Masters naturally rated Billy in the top ten most dangerous players in the finals.

> The Melbourne fullback has led the NRL the past three seasons for the most number of runs and metres gained from returning the ball from an opposition kick.

Despite the Storm's inconsistent form for most of the competition season, Slater made 156 attacking runs for 1497 m. Slater has hands the size of a baby octopus, meaning he can pluck a rolling ball off the ground or seize it from the air and carry it one-handed, fending off would-be defenders. Slater thrills Melbourne's AFL-educated public more than any player in the NRL.

From the early days, Masters was a big fan of Billy's. Masters got to meet him at close hand when he went down to the Storm at the invitation of Bellamy to give a few speeches on football tactics to the players. He thought Billy was the ultimate player and 'a class bloke off the field'.

Earlier on in his career Masters compared Billy to young Swans player Lewis Roberts-Thomson. He said both 'have a cool moniker and a warm smile', and both shared incredible skills from an early age. Masters believed Billy would have made it in the AFL.

In the first two finals matches, the Storm disposed of Manly and then Brisbane in similar high-scoring victories. Billy scored 4 tries in the demolition of the premiers Manly, 1 try off a Smith grubber, and another off an Inglis run and fend to wow the Etihad Stadium crowd. Billy did another great grubber and chase to score against Brisbane to land another 2 tries (videos later showed he'd scored a third try but the referee refused to review it and he was told to play the ball). Billy had scored 6 tries in two finals games, one of the best efforts ever by an NRL player. (He added another one in the grand final to make it 7 tries in three games.) It set up a great contest with Parramatta, and most tantalisingly, the match-up between two of the hottest players in league, Billy and Jarryd Hayne. Hayne was in superlative form.

Grand final day didn't have a smooth start for Hayne. He'd brought two left boots (both bright red) to the stadium. Eels' officials hurriedly arranged a police escort to get through the grand final crowd to retrieve Hayne's missing right boot from the Eels hotel in time for the kick-off.

An early hitch off the field was replicated on the field as the Eels failed to find their feet in the first half in front of 82,000 people at ANZ Stadium. Parramatta seemed in awe of the moment even though the bulk of supporters were pumping for the blue and yellow. The Eels hadn't been in a grand final since 2001, and hadn't won a grand final since 1986. The Storm were in familiar territory—it was their fourth consecutive grand final appearance. The Storm led 10–0 at half-time after tries to Hoffman and Blair. Billy was working off Cronk the whole time, punching holes in the Eels defence on the left in the first half, then in the second half he started attacking the Eels through the right-side. He was putting in a man-of-the-match performance.

Parramatta hit back with an early try but then Inglis, as he so often did on the big occasions, went into overdrive, plucking the ball high in the air from a superbly weighted Cronk bomb to score. Billy then added to the scoreline with a try running off an inside pass. The Storm screamed away to a 22–6 scoreline. Parramatta hit back with 2 late tries but despite a gallant effort, they ran out of time. The Storm were always just in control, always with a timely buffer and when they needed that extra point at the end to put Parramatta out of business, Inglis again stepped up to the plate and plonked a field goal. Melbourne had their third premiership.

Billy was named best on ground and was awarded the prestigious Clive Churchill Medal. He humbly said he felt Cooper Cronk deserved it more than he did.

Slater told his Storm buddies: 'To my boys tonight, I thought this should go to Cooper, you boys are unbelievable and I love you to death.'

Later, one of the judges, Souths legend Bob McCarthy, said he thought Billy had an outstanding game and deserved the award, despite an error by Billy late in the game that almost gifted the Eels try—after a bomb by his rival Hayne.

McCarthy told *The Sydney Morning Herald*:

> I know he said Cooper should have won it, but I think he was just trying to look after his mates. We have four judges and I think they're pretty good judges of a game of football. We were unanimous on it. That was our opinion Billy had an exceptional game. He was smashed to pieces a few times, put his body on the line, got his try, ran all day and made a lot of metres. We thought he was outstanding. So was Cooper Cronk, Ryan Hoffman ... a few of them. Billy dropped that bomb off [Jarryd] Hayne at the end but it went so high no-one would have caught it with all the traffic around him.

McCarthy said there was a history of Churchill Medal winners saying they didn't deserve the honour, while debate raged in the public about who should have got it. 'Craig Fitzgibbon was the same when he won it. He said he didn't deserve it, too. But he'd been fantastic. He got up and said Brad Fittler should have won it. They get modest. If I was Billy, I wouldn't care what anyone said. I'd take it, give it a kiss and get off the stage.'

There was someone else who could smile—Finch. He was told by Parramatta earlier in the year he had 'no future'. Now he had a premiership ring. After jumping ship he'd beaten his old team in a grand final. His future couldn't look any brighter.

Smith made out the Storm was anxious at the end. 'I was going to call for the trainer to get a change of Speedos,' joked Smith later. Smith, of course, was exaggerating. 'It was exciting the first time we won,' said Smith. 'But there's a real sense of achievement this year.'

Billy seemed certain of being named in the Australian team to play in the Four Nations tournament in Britain. He told Channel Nine: 'Hopefully it will be exciting to go over there and play.'

Billy wore the medal in the Storm dressing room while Tyla, now eleven months, sat on his knee. Billy had all his family around—just as he always did for the big occasions.

Several hours after the win the Storm players, after a few quiet beers, gathered in the middle of the Stadium to talk about their great effort. They were all dressed in their Storm suits. Bellamy had collected the team together. It was an unusual gathering for a grand final. They were almost the last people at the ground. Normally the serious talks happen *before* the game. They talked about what they had achieved and where they were headed. Smith spoke and told them 'look around, appreciate the moment, and if you're willing to do the hard work and improve no matter what's in front of you, you're capable'. It was like Bellamy was stilling the emotion inside them for a while, steeling them for what was ahead. They had no idea the real storm was raging all round them and about to bring their club to its knees, make them feel sick in the stomach and feel dirty on the game. There were many huddles to follow in the next year. For now it was all glory and bright futures.

The Storm went back to the nearby Acer Arena a short while later to celebrate the victory with almost 5000 fans and invited guests. The sound mixer played AC/DC's 'Thunderstruck' as the Storm players took centre stage, one player crowd surfing, and wearing dress-up gear and wigs, sporting Storm 2009 premiers T-shirts. Billy hugged Bellamy and showed off the Storm scarf to the crowd. Smith said the team had had a few quiet beers after the game and had no idea such a big crowd was waiting for them at the after-match party. 'There were 70,000 people in yellow and blue shirts in the stadium today but we showed them,' Smith said. There was a huge cheer and the party raged on.

The next day the Storm arrived for the post-grand final celebration with fans at Princes Park in North Carlton back in Melbourne. Billy was sporting the Clive Churchill Medal and all the players were wearing their premiership rings. The microphone was handed round among the players and they got to address the Storm's purple army.

Billy said:

> To be honest the build-up seemed pretty similar to the 2007 grand final. In 2007 we felt pretty confident and we felt the same going into the grand final with Parramatta. We started the game really well, we pretty much smothered Parramatta in defence and we shut down all their options. The second half we didn't start too well and gave them a bit of a sniff but we hung in there and we showed we are a great side.

Billy was obviously a crowd favourite and got the biggest cheer. He seemed composed and in his element. Four days later he was named the Storm player of the year for the second year in a row.

Billy didn't have long to get his feet on the ground. He was named in the Australian squad for the Four Nations tournament and was soon off to Britain and France for the six-week tour. It was a busy time for him. He had proposed to Nicole and they were due to be married in Cairns on 28 November.

The first game of the tournament was slotted in for 24 October in London where Australia was to take on their old rival New Zealand. They were still smarting from the World Cup victory. In a dour struggle, the game ended in a 20–all draw with neither Hayne nor Billy starring. Billy had won the number one jersey and Hayne, just voted the best player in the world, was on the wing. Billy was happy to have the classy Hayne in the team and had pushed for his inclusion.

Australia rebounded in the next game defeating England, with Billy scoring 2 tries in the 26–16 win at Wigan. New

Zealand were then knocked out of the tournament when England ran over them to set up a final with Australia at Leeds on 14 November.

England came out of the blocks on their home soil and lock 'Slammin' Sam Burgess ran through the Australian defence, including Billy, to score. England led 10–6 after twenty minutes and there was no sign of the impending Australian flood of tries. Australia led just 14–10 at half-time.

It was then Billy starred on the field and, as many commentators said, erased the terrible memories of the 2008 World Cup final. Billy was all over the English and they couldn't hold him. He was having a ball in front of the 31,000 English fans at Elland Road, who suddenly saw any hope of an English league resurgence thrown out the window. Billy made a spectacular run for the ball over the English try line, knocked it up and then, leaping over the dead ball line, knocked it back into the arms of captain Smith, who scored. Billy raced in another 2 tries as the Kangaroos over-ran the English 46–16. Storm players had scored half of Australia's tries.

Asked how it compared to his World Cup brain fade, Billy joked: 'About 90 metres was the difference. There you go.'

In the Four Nations final Billy had turned everything around. Instead of possibly wrecking momentum, he created it, and had changed the game in Australia's favour; instead of losing the ball, he held it and when he flew over the sideline he popped it back into his team's hands, not the opposition's. Billy had just played his natural game and this time it had worked. It was amazing what a difference one game can make to a reputation.

'Last year's last year—you can't change that. As a player, you've just got to get over it and move on. I feel that this team and everyone in it has moved on. The Kiwis are the World Cup holders and we're the Four Nations holders now.'

The *Yorkshire Evening Post* lamented England's performance when they suffered 'yet another lesson at the hands of Australia'. The *Post* reported:

> The Kangaroos have been dominant for the best part of four decades and, despite some encouraging signs, England seem as far behind as ever. England led three times, were ahead as late as the fifty-fourth minute and only a converted try adrift with thirteen to go. But Australia's greater class eventually told, four late unanswered tries leaving the hosts battered, bewildered and well-beaten. Fullback Billy Slater capped a wonderful performance with a hat-trick of tries.

* * *

The clouds had lifted on Billy's international career, and when he was jetting home to Australia, his family was praying the clouds would also lift for Billy and Nicole's upcoming wedding in the Far North. It was the rainy season and the family were dicing with the weather gods for the big day on 28 November.

Woman's Day bought exclusive rights to the wedding, which was staged in Nicole's mother's garden in Cairns. *Women's Day* didn't count on a wily *Cairns Post* (News

Limited) photographer sneaking some shots through the fence as Billy and Nicole held hands alongside the marriage celebrant, ruining the *Woman's Day* exclusive. News Limited had crashed the wedding for *Woman's Day*. What was supposed to be a three-page colourful spread on the couple in the magazine ended up as just a short one-page piece.

Woman's Day reporter Warren Gibbs said the wedding day was beautiful, the weather had cleared, and he was made to feel right at home. The newlyweds were taken up to the Cairns hinterland for some wedding shots while the guests—everyone from Billy's Storm teammates to his early boyhood friends—enjoyed the wedding feast, which included a pig on a spit. Bellamy was also there to see his charge tie the knot. Billy said it was a celebration of his life with Nicole, rather than a traditional wedding.

It was a perfect end to a perfect year.

CHAPTER ELEVEN

CAUGHT IN A STORM

Normally before a storm arrives there are warning signs: a rise in temperature, swirling clouds, even a sudden stillness. The air grows heavy and sultry and then the sky slowly blackens. But when the salary cap crisis hit Melbourne it was like a bolt from the blue.

Early in the year, on 11 January, Storm chief Waldron resigned to take up a position with the new rugby franchise, the Melbourne Rebels. It was a sudden departure. Observers brushed it off as perhaps Waldron wanting to go out on a high after a premiership win. Little did they know the mess he was leaving behind.

In late March, *The Sun-Herald* broke a story revealing the Storm were being investigated for alleged salary cap breaches. The story centred on captain Cameron Smith and his tie in with Fox Sports in a $45,000-a-year third-party deal. But it could all be explained, or possibly settled, and it wasn't a massive breach, if it was a breach at all. The Storm had been fined before for breaches not much smaller. It didn't seem it would envelop the whole club. It was business between one News Limited company and another. Surely News Limited knew their own business?

March and April brought some strange ides. You didn't need a guy on a mat with some ancient marbles for fortune-telling to see something was up when certain punters put bets on the premiers Melbourne to take out the wooden spoon. Some punters were scooping up odds of 300–1. It was very strange betting behaviour. It was a bit like busy ants signalling approaching rain. But the signs were tiny.

The Storm had started the season as normal, on a high. They'd won their first four games and were leading the ladder again. By mid-April there were worrying indications when they lost the next two games. Was something foul afoot? Were rumours trickling down from management to the ranks that a hard rain was going to fall?

It all came blazingly clear on Thursday 22 April when all hell broke loose and the thunderbolt struck. The sky darkened and the worst day in the club's history unfolded. It came with a thrashing rain and was relentless. No-one could escape the fury.

Storm executive (acting CEO) Matt Hanson, News Limited connected director Craig Watt and board chairman Dr Rob Moodie attended a crisis meeting at NRL headquarters in Sydney on the Thursday morning with News Limited and NRL executives. They'd been warned in a letter of the impending findings and the Storm were urged to disclose their knowledge of the salary cap rorts (Moodie and Watt denied and were later cleared by News Limited of any involvement in the salary cap breaches). It was explained to them that huge salary cap breaches had been detected dating back almost five years. The breaches ran into almost $1.7 million. The case against some of the office holders was gathered by Ian Schubert, the salary cap auditor, and also from information supplied by undisclosed sources outside the club. NRL chief David Gallop claimed the Storm had kept two sets of books, with three players getting side letters promising extra payments. The club was told it would face the toughest of sanctions, which would be revealed to the public later in the day. The Storm would be stripped of their 2007 and 2009 premierships and their minor premierships of 2006, 2007 and 2008, have to repay more than $1 million in prize money, be fined $500,000, and then be forced to play for no points for the rest of the season. It was blow after blow after blow. It was like an angry father punishing a bewildered son. The Storm executives stood there in disbelief at the penalties and at their predicament.

The news slowly filtered back to Storm headquarters. The players were warned of the impending public announcement by Gallop and News Limited chief John Hartigan.

When the penalties were relayed to Bellamy, he just sat behind his desk at Storm headquarters and buried his head in his hands. He couldn't move. It seemed like the greatest things he had achieved in his professional life had been taken away from him he would tell them in the dressing shed at training that afternoon.

The Storm players, including Billy, bunkered down to work through the crisis. They started ringing friends and wives asking what they should do. They didn't even know if they would be playing on the weekend in the scheduled match against the Warriors. Some didn't even know if they would be playing footy again.

Nicole Rose had a heart-to-heart with Billy as it all unfolded. 'Play for no points? Why would you put your body on the line for that?,' she asked him. Billy was so shocked. He didn't want to speak to anyone. He'd taken more than a few knocks in his career but this one had come right out of left field. He was one of the players that hadn't signed any secret agreement. He knew nothing about how the third-party agreements were being paid and met. And he couldn't understand why the club and players were taking the blame for a rotten administration.

Billy told Steve Mascord:

> The biggest fear for me, initially when it all went down, was 'was that it for this club, had we played our last game for the Melbourne Storm?' Like, it was so big. It was shocking news. The feeling in that little shed we were in when we got told, the emotion from our coach, it was pretty shattering. Walking out of that room, we didn't know what was going to happen. We were days out from playing against the Warriors. I didn't know whether that game was going to take place, I didn't know whether the rest of the season [was going to happen].

Cooper Cronk was sick in the stomach. He told a close friend he was fed up with rugby league, he wanted to walk from the game. He was totally dirty on the whole thing.

Five-eighth Gareth Widdop had only just joined the top ranks of the Storm. The English-born player, who had migrated to Australia at the age of sixteen with his family, had risen up through the ranks of Victorian rugby league and the Storm feeder system only to find his first class debut year was taken away from him. He was bewildered, but prepared to give his best for the Storm. He was due to make his debut on the Sunday against the Warriors.

'We all sat around and said. "Why are we doing this, why are we playing for no points?"' Widdop remembers.

Bellamy had to do something to keep it all together. Hartigan had rung Bellamy and wanted to know if the coach was aware of the rorting. Bellamy said he had no idea. Hartigan took his word for it. Bellamy had to pick up the broken pieces from the fall-out and remuster the troops. The whole club was at risk of falling apart. He needed to find a gel to keep his troops together amid the crisis. He called for a team leader meeting at assistant coach Stephen Kearney's home the next morning. He told the group, in which various people kept coming in and out, including News Limited and Storm executives, that they needed to find some strength of purpose. After hours of talking they eventually, in their heart of hearts, found the commitment to play on, but they needed a reason to play. They hooked on to the idea of playing each game for a charity.

The crisis couldn't have come at a worse time for the city fathers of Melbourne helping to back the Storm. The Storm were set to help unveil the new multi-purpose AAMI Stadium, the first major rectangular stadium in Melbourne, that would host rugby league, rugby and soccer. It was supposed to be a time of celebration, not humiliation.

Even number one supporter Molly Meldrum, who was in strife-torn Thailand at the time, was lost for words and worried that the club would never recover. Meldrum said the loss of the premiership flags would kill the club. 'I'm in Bangkok covering the red revolution and it's explosive, getting worse by the minute,' Meldrum said. 'It's all about passion with the red shirts, the yellow shirts, the army and the government. It's imploding. And now when I look at what's happening at home, my entire team I love, that being Melbourne Storm, has imploded in a minute. How can we recover from this?'

The Storm's first chief Chris Johns flew down to inspire the players to stay true to the club.

> I spoke to them and said one of the greatest compliments they'd received was from Collingwood coach Mick Malthouse. He'd commented that of all the clubs he'd seen, the Melbourne Storm stood out as a club where the individuals put their own aims aside for the club. He respected them for the way they honoured their club. I told them that was a huge feather in their cap coming from someone like Malthouse.

The Storm were due to train the next day at the new stadium and there was an agreement that everyone would show up and keep a strong face when a press conference was held afterwards. Ribot agreed to come down and gave them a supportive talk before they faced the media.

In what league reporters say was one of the most moving and electric moments they had seen in their career, Bellamy came walking across the stadium ground towards the waiting press with a phalanx of Storm players in their proud shirts behind him. They all looked straight ahead and determined. No-one blinked. Bellamy told the media that the players were aggrieved and had no knowledge of the salary cap rorts. They vowed to play on.

Bellamy told the press the players were gutted and what they cherished most had been taken away from them. 'These players love our club. This club is a great club, it's a strong club, it's a very proud club. It also has been a successful club. This is why we stand here today united. We are not going anywhere. We ain't gonna surrender. We will stand up for ourselves and we will fight our way back from here. That fight starts today and tomorrow it starts on the field.'

It was strong stuff. Bellamy was told to expect a raft of questions. Instead there was just dumbfounded silence. Somehow the journalists knew this was not the moment to probe and prod, these were deeply hurt people.

Against all the odds, the next day at Etihad Stadium the Storm lived up to their words. They thrashed the Warriors 40–6. Smith said it was one of the team's greatest victories given the circumstances. 'I think the thing that drove us most was our pride and our passion for the club and there wasn't a chance in hell that we weren't going to give our best performance.'

Bellamy was defiant too. 'We've had a lot taken away from us in the last two or three days but they are not going to take our spirit away,' he said. 'We've had something taken off us ... They can cross our names out of the record books but they can't take from our heart that we know that we deserved those grand final [wins] and that is not going to change.'

There was lingering anger and bewilderment. The wives and partners at home were still coming to terms with the punishment, and there was more to follow. News Limited had announced a further forensic investigation into the salary cap breaches and a new axe would hang over the team for a couple of months. Payments to eight players were under the microscope. Already the club was $700,000 over the salary cap just for 2010.

The wolves started gathering around the damaged club. News Limited had indicated it was inevitable the Storm would lose some of its top players in order to stay within the $4.1 million salary cap. The Broncos were hungry to pick up a few of the players, especially if Folau, as expected, left its fold for an AFL career. Billy was high on the Broncos shopping list. There was also talk the new rugby franchise, the Melbourne Rebels, might poach some of the Storm stars, including Billy, but there had been an agreement the previous year that each club wouldn't poach from the other. AFL teams were also expressing interest in getting Billy.

Smith said he wouldn't be going anywhere, no matter what the offer. Billy was staying firm too. Inglis seemed the most likely person to leave, with his desire to reunite with family in Queensland.

Anger built up as the season progressed. All of the players vowed they would never return any of their premiership rings. Ronnie Slater declared: 'as far as Billy is concerned he won those two premierships.' Ribot was livid at the treatment of his former club. He said the penalties dished out were 'the greatest acts of injustice in the history of Australian sport'. He said all the players were denied natural justice. Suddenly his favourite team had hit 'a submerged log' and was sinking.

He revealed he'd tried at the last minute to persuade Gallop not to take the premierships off the team:

> They [the NRL and News Limited] put one and one together and got ten and decided to eat their [the Storm's] arms and legs off. I rang David and said 'there's no way you can do that [take the premierships away], you have to follow the process through'. But they had made their minds up that that was appropriate.
>
> When Hartigan came down [to Melbourne] threatening to send people to jail I thought that was outrageous there. I don't know why or how they came up with that. It was just that Brian Waldron got lazy with the treatment of things and for his laziness people had to pay the ultimate price. All natural justice was denied to them [the players].

The club was built on its culture, and here News Limited was saying the culture was rotten at its core. Hartigan came down to Melbourne later in July with all guns blazing. News Limited had enlisted accountants Deloitte to unravel the trail of rorts. The forensic accountants had sorted through 160,000 documents.

Hartigan called Waldron the chief rat of the rorts. 'He's the architect of this whole badness in this club,' said Hartigan. 'And I also suggested at another level that there were rats in the ranks. I think it's quite simple, if you draw a line between both of those comments I think it leads to the chief rat, and I have no question or doubt that it's him.'

Hartigan said the other rats were Matt Hanson, Peter Gregory, Cameron Vale and Peter O'Sullivan. 'Our original suspicion was that there was an elaborate and well-orchestrated deception by senior management at the club and that has been confirmed by the Deloitte investigation.' He said the findings of the Deloitte report would be referred to police. 'Is it fraud? That's something for the police to decide,' he said. (No criminal or other actions followed from the inquiries. Waldron threatened to sue for defamation over the claims that the breaches involved a fraud.)

Deloitte were unable to interview any of the players about the issues they uncovered, which included Storm paying for a $30,000 boat to Greg Inglis. The audit found Inglis was paid more than $200,000 more than the $400,000 deal former chief Waldron had registered with the NRL. Inglis had also been given a voucher to buy goods from Storm sponsor Harvey Norman. As a marquee player he was entitled to these benefits, to earn up to $150,000, but Storm had not declared the arrangements with the NRL. Both Inglis and his manager Allan Gainey protested they had no knowledge that the information was not passed on to the NRL. (Players can obtain outside sponsors as long as they do not conflict with other Storm sponsors. These agreements have to be ticked off by both the club and the NRL.)

News Limited said in its release: 'The main method of payment involved the club arranging for third parties to "employ" and/or pay players. The third parties issued invoices to the club for amounts described as "donations" or "consulting fees". The club paid the invoices and they were recorded in the accounts as "donations" or "consulting fees" and not as payments to players.'

News Limited insisted taking away the premierships was appropriate considering the size of the salary cap breaches:

> There have been media reports that people associated with the club believe the NRL should reinstate the 2007 premiership, based on a belief that the estimated breach of the salary cap in 2007 was about $273,000. Those calling for the reinstatement of the 2007 premiership have noted that the club's salary cap breach in 2007 was similar to the breach by the club in 2003 of $261,912 and that the penalty for that breach was a fine of only $130,956. Following the forensic investigation, it is News Limited's view that the actual breach in 2007 was an estimated $551,032, 110 per cent higher than the breach in 2003.

> Similarly, News Limited now believes that the actual breach in 2009 when the Storm won the premiership was an estimated $964,877, higher again than the breach in 2007. Combined with the fact that the breaches occurred over five years, the findings made by Deloitte reinforce News Limited's view that the penalties were appropriate.

Hartigan said: 'These are tough penalties that affect many people in the Storm family who have done absolutely nothing wrong. This includes the fans, employees and many, many players. These people have shown extraordinary loyalty and support over the past three months. The club spirit has been simply outstanding, and I thank them for that.'

But he said the Storm had to take its medicine.

As the salary rorts crisis continued to roll on during the year, the senior players in the team were still called on to play at state and international level.

Cooper Cronk was delighted in May when he won his first Australian jersey to join Inglis, Smith and Billy to play New Zealand. It was everything that he wanted to achieve in league and it helped heal the great wound he was carrying from the crisis. (Cronk helped Australia win 12–8.) Cronk was on the bench when the quartet again starred in another Origin series victory for Queensland, Billy scoring the deciding try in the last dead-rubber game and being named man of the match. It was Bellamy's last hurrah as the Blues Origin coach after three straight series defeats.

Bellamy lamented the lack of enthusiasm from his Blues players in Origin game one, which New South Wales only lost by four points. He said he looked inside himself and found he had no answers as how to turn the Blues mental attitude around. 'I think some players are more suited to club footy than representative footy, and some coaches are more suited to representative footy than club footy. I am more suited to club coaching,' he said in his book, *Home Truths*.

At least he wouldn't have to feel again that torn heart of training against his elite Storm players in the Maroons team.

The Storm, though, were winning the mental game. Bellamy was a good friend of *Sydney Morning Herald* journalist Roy Masters, who often gave the Storm motivational speeches during the season. The former coach was one of the most knowledgeable tacticians in the game. Masters had learnt from previous experience there was no point adopting a negative attitude after adversity.

Masters had famously started the 'fibros versus silvertails' mentality when he was coaching Western Suburbs and they were taking on Manly. 'I tried that "them and us" philosophy and it didn't work. I told Craig there was no good in making out enemies. The best way forward was to exploit your strengths. You have to be expansive, not negative. You don't want to get yourself bound up in negative forces,' Masters told Bellamy.

Masters took great pride in watching the Storm slowly come out from the depths of despair. They might have lost the bottom line game with accountants but they were winning the mental game.

Chris Johns also noted how the team accepted their predicament. Each week they had to look at the competition table and see they were sixteenth. But they knuckled down to wanting to make amends in the following years.

'I believe they were extremely hard done by,' said Johns. 'And they had to go out each week and play for no points and often get booed or called cheats. It was amazingly unfair.'

The fact they were being so competitive during the season showed 'what an amazing player group' they were, Johns said. All kinds of offers were being made to players to desert the Storm. Billy was at one stage linked to a bid from Eddie Jones to get him to play rugby union in Japan for $750,000 a season.

'I'm sure a lot of those players including Cam and Billy could have got a lot more money playing somewhere else, but in a sense they took a pay cut, rolled up their sleeves and got the place moving again,' Johns said.

Looking back on the crisis a few years later, Billy said:

> The initial fear was: was the club going to fold and where were we going to sit, what were we going to do? But, yeah, looking back on it, the club's got some pretty strong people in it. You just have to look at guys who have stuck around and still have roles, like Robbie Kearns and Peter Robinson ... who are really the heart and soul of this club and have created the culture here.
>
> It's a part of my history, it's a part of the club's history. You are always going to have the memories of going through it. I think it's how you come out the other

side, how you handle yourself in those situations. I'm certainly comfortable with what I've done. I've put it behind me enough to move on. I think the club has done a great job and the people in the club have done a great job of getting through the situation we were in.

The club reluctantly parted with a number of club favourites before the season—Steve Turner, Dallas Johnson, Joseph Tomane, Matt Cross, Aidan Guerra and Will Chambers—in a bid to keep its marquee players. At the end of the season, Inglis also said he was going, leaving for the Broncos (that deal subsequently broke down and Inglis ended up at Souths).

In one of the last games of the season the Storm, as they normally did, ran over the Raiders, this time 36–12. They were still showing plenty of motivation in August.

Smith said it had been tough. 'There are days when you don't really feel like coming in here and training or having to do the hard work,' he said.

Bellamy had noticed how the team was getting back into its old groove and the emotions were calming down. 'They've been a lot more receptive to getting back to how we have run things in the past, that's been good for us,' he said. 'It's hard to enjoy your footy 100 per cent when you are playing for nothing.'

Many Storm supporters, though, were shaken. They felt they'd been duped and the salary cap crisis had revealed an inner emptiness in the club. The Storm were struggling even to top the smallest crowds who attended AFL games. Storm supporter Michael Winkler wrote in *The Age*:

> They cannot win anything other than the wooden spoon, but the only guaranteed winners of the competition are the major media companies and the NRL. Clubs are franchises. Tradition and history are commodities. I don't believe Storm will be around in five years' time, and that will be sad for my sons who believe that they are the club and the club is them. I will just enjoy it while it lasts. And, at some point, Slater will loom at prop Jeff Lima's shoulder, take an offload and slice through the opposition's monolithic forwards, and that will be magnificent to watch, just as it always is.

But it was not the death knell. Melbourne was made of stronger stuff.

Billy had survived the storm. And he had also achieved two major awards during the year, despite not being able to play for a point with his club. He won the Wally Lewis Medal for the best Queensland player in Origin and also the Dally M Award for representative player of the year. He helped Australia get to the top of the Four Nations tournament table later in the year, although Australia were defeated in the final by New Zealand.

Billy had something even more special to celebrate from his year—the birth of his son Jake. Whatever had happened at the Storm, life was cruising along in the Slater home. Nicole was gaining new commissions for her art and their friendships among other Storm players were keeping them happy in Melbourne. Everyone was looking forward to putting the pain of 2010 behind them.

'I have a little girl and a baby boy,' Billy once said proudly. 'You talk about priorities, my kids and my wife Nicole are mine. They're the people who make life great when things are a bit tough.'

CHAPTER TWELVE

RESURRECTION

If anyone wants to know how to dust off their shoes and walk on after a major setback, they need look no further than how Billy put his mind to work and bagged a booty of awards after the misery of the salary cap crisis.

Not only did he bounce back with confidence from such a huge blow—losing two premierships and three minor premierships—but he also came back from shoulder surgery during the pre-season. He missed training for most of the pre-season and could only watch on as his teammates were revved up for the reality of the competition after their surreal and dismal year of 2010.

He carried the shoulder injury late into the year and then went through the tough rigours of a Four Nations tournament.

As always, Billy didn't make a big deal of the problem. 'It's in a better spot than what it was last year when I was playing, so put it that way,' he said.

After giving his shoulder a workout in the Storm's traditional pre-season wrestling sessions, which he flew through, he knew he was on course to start the year.

He'd come out of the miserable year with a new sense of relief. Although he was playing for no points, he found his joy of the game had returned. With the pressure off, he'd recharged. 'I think that freshened me up mentally because you can get into the whole grind of things after nine years at the top level. It can become a chore. We just got back to playing for the love of the game,' he said.

He was about to produce one of his most scintillating and consistent years of football and be duly acknowledged at home and abroad. The crisis had spurred him to play even better. That was Billy: ever seeking to improve. When he received his award for best footballer in the world, he just said he wanted to improve for each new game, he didn't have time to look back.

He'd left the dark days of the Storm's pointless year for a splash of orange. New boots with moulded studs that suited his playing mode arrived in bright orange. He thought of toning down to another colour but daughter Tyla took a shine to them. 'There's daddy in his orange boots,' she'd shout at the games. She loved watching him play. Billy felt he couldn't let her down and change the colour.

Not only did he help Melbourne to a minor premiership (one that couldn't be taken off them), but he also helped Queensland to a seventh straight Origin victory and then helped steer Australia to a Four Nations victory, although a broken collarbone ruled him out of the final. Billy was everywhere and in everything.

He was voted the best player in Australia in winning the Dally M Medal, and then he was voted the best player in the world by the Rugby League International Federation at a gala dinner at the Tower of London during the Four Nations tournament.

'After a game people might be talking about a try I scored, or a run I made, or a catch I took. But I might be thinking about the tackle I missed, or the pass I should have given to the winger, or something like that. As a rugby league player, you are always thinking of the negative side. But I am aware of what people go to the football for, and why they enjoy watching myself play,' he said.

But in a sense that was his positive attitude. He didn't dwell on wins and losses, he worked to get over the issues, to rise above them.

It didn't happen by accident. He was one of the most dedicated at training in the competition. Everyone noted how he always loosened down after a training session. He'd nearly always be the last one to leave.

Although he often lived on his instincts and reactions, he'd also become a keen student of the game. He knew how to set a defensive line, when to chime in, always scouting at the back and ready for an opportunity.

The legends of the game noted his abilities and many of them rated him as one of the best of all time.

Former Balmain fullback Keith Barnes said Billy was in the same ilk as legends Clive Churchill and Graeme Langlands.

'I rate him in the same class,' Barnes told *The Sun-Herald* after Billy won the Dally M Award. 'Billy is sensational. He has flair in attack, his anticipation is great, he reads the game and his defence is first class—he has everything.'

When people say why they admire Billy, the one thing they often say is that they 'just love to watch him play.' He brings that air of excitement like all great players when he is on the field. His unpredictability, his flair—such attributes are great crowd pullers.

One of the immortals, Bob Fulton, Manly and Australia's great halfback and a major part of the Blues Origin squad for many years, has seen Billy all too often cut up New South Wales. Fulton said he hates rating players from one generation to another, but in Billy's generation in league, he can't think of a more supreme athlete. 'He is a freak of a player. He is seriously special, and what's more he's a tremendous athlete. He didn't win *Australia's Greatest Athlete* by accident.' Whether he's playing for the Storm, Queensland or Australia, he comes up with the clutch plays that gets a team back on board and gets them a win. 'He knows the game backwards. I couldn't put a big enough rap on him and I'd pay anything to go and see him play.'

Langlands had his view on the bloke everyone compares to him: 'I haven't seen Billy Slater play a bad game, and I watch most games every weekend. His attack play is very, very good. He's done everything right. It's impossible to make comparisons between eras because the game has changed so dramatically, but he's by far the best fullback going around. He's great.'

Dally Messenger III said Billy has the X-factor. 'He has that extra edge. I have Dally's scrapbooks, and when you read some of the reports you think, "Could he really have done that?" But Billy proves he could have, because he's done some phenomenal things on the field. I see him as the greatest living example of my grandfather's profile.'

Another early fan of Billy's is the famous Essendon coach Kevin Sheedy. Sheedy used to get a seat in the stands at Storm games with his mate and fellow AFL legend Tom Hafey to watch Billy display his amazing skills on the field. 'In my opinion he is a superstar,' says Sheedy. Sheedy had little knowledge of league but what he saw in Billy amazed him: his all-round skills, speed off the mark and ball handling. He had all the ball skills of an AFL player—and that critical 360 degree ability to move from one position. Sheedy eventually coached one of Billy's team-mates Israel Folau, one of the AFL's great marketing coups. 'Folau was gettable for us [when Sheedy coached Greater Western Sydney and signed Folau] and he could take the high mark.' Sheedy says he knows of no offer being given to Billy to change codes, although he saw him as an ideal AFL player. 'Billy is just a legend in his own game. When I was sitting there with Tommy watching Billy, I said "this guy is unbelievable"—his speed, his decision-making and his courage. I thought he'd be good in anything he played. The only thing I thought he wouldn't be any good at was as a goalie in soccer!'

Bellamy never held back his admiration for Billy. He said 'Immortal' Graeme Langlands was his favourite player as a kid. 'I didn't see Clive Churchill, I must say,' Bellamy said.

'But there was Langlands, Graham Eadie, Garry Jack, Gary Belcher, but I must say I don't think I've seen a better fullback before. No I haven't.'

Senior sports journalist Brent Read rates Billy as the best fullback he has seen: 'When they look back at who were the greatest of this generation they will say Cam [Smith], Billy, Thurston and Inglis. They are a vintage bunch. Billy's the best I've seen and many people I know rate him as the best fullback the game's ever seen. He's such a good ball player now and strong in defence. He's just turned himself into the complete footballer.'

ABC *Grandstand*'s Debbie Spillane said Billy was not just the best fullback, but the best player she had seen. Spillane was commentating for the ABC on the sideline in a game between the Storm and the Dragons when she had a close-up look at Billy in action. Debbie Spillane writing for *The Roar*:

> The big deal for me was it would be my first chance to observe from close quarters the player I regard as the best I've ever seen in rugby league: Billy Slater.
>
> When the Storm have the ball, Slater is still in organising mode. Pointing, shouting, calling plays and when he slots into the backline he does so with a precise purpose—there's something on, and he might be going to help set it up or to finish it off. Or a bit of both. Or, on occasion, he might be just keeping the defence nervous by 'looming' as the great Jack Gibson used to call it.
>
> When Slater chimes into the attack he's not just joining in on the off-chance that something might be

on. When Slater gets involved something is on and quite often it looks like he's called it.

He can bust open a defence like Eadie, Thornett or Langlands, read the play and set up others like a Belcher or Lockyer, defend like Jack, judge where to turn up in support like Johns, handle the high ball like Fairfax or Brentnall and run tryline to tryline beating defenders with a combo of devastating acceleration, evasive skills and sheer sustained pace to score like Mullins. That makes him not just the best fullback the modern game has ever seen, but someone who is equal to or better than every other fullback in living memory in whatever the strongest facet of their play was.

I don't know that any other star player in any other position on the field has his major all-time rivals covered in such a way.

Many observers marvel at Billy's ability to change gears and his amazing pace off the mark. His ability to move from a standing start is almost beyond equal in all major football codes. He can go from a slow pace to a quick pace in a nanosecond.

Conditioning coach Jock Campbell said: 'His acceleration over 10–30 metres is unbelievable and his maximum speed is as good as anyone. But one of the things that really sets him apart is how he can change gears. He can go from second to fifth gear in a couple of steps and there are few blokes in history who can do that.'

Steve Mascord has covered rugby league for more than twenty-five years and said Billy is definitely the best fullback he's ever seen. He said one of his unacknowledged strengths is how well he starts a season. While many players have to run themselves into form, Billy starts with a wing on each foot. 'I don't know if it is something he works on in the pre-seasons but I've seen it in the challenge cup games in England, everyone is surprised how much form he is in,' Mascord said. (The league club challenge is between the top English and top Australian sides from the previous year and is normally staged in England around February, just before the Australian league season kicks off.)

Mascord has seen Billy's prickly side too. He hated to talk about his rival for Australian fullback, Brett Stewart, and brushed off questions Mascord asked him about Stewart.

Age sports journalist Stathi Paxinos also encountered Billy's prickly side during his long period covering the Storm. Once, when he questioned Billy about his year of suspensions, Billy walked out of the interview. Other journalists turned to Paxinos and asked 'What happened there?' 'I don't know he just got upset,' Paxinos replied.

Paxinos copped a spray once from Bellamy in front of the whole Storm training squad over an article Paxinos had written in *The Age* in which he quoted Robbie Kearns saying Billy had let the side down with his long list of suspensions in 2006. Bellamy was upset Paxinos had gone to Kearns, who now held an administrative role at the Storm after his playing career. The verbal barrage was confronting for Paxinos, but he still respected Bellamy for what he had achieved with the team.

Paxinos saw more of the siege mentality at work at the Storm. He found they often bunkered down under the attacks from other clubs, and he felt this occurred after the salary cap crisis, when certain members of the media were excluded from the inner sanctum. He believes Bellamy's sense of purpose was critical to reviving the Storm after 2010.

Billy was not keen to do interviews. Once, *The Sydney Morning Herald*'s Brad Walter and other journalists were forced to wait for more than an hour to speak to Billy after a State of Origin game in Melbourne when they were eager to meet their deadlines. 'He has this kind of disdain for the media,' said Walter.

One journalist who has always had a good working relationship with Billy is Karl de Kroo, then with the *Herald-Sun*. De Kroo was there when Billy kicked off his career and always found him approachable. 'A few journos found him a little difficult at times but I always had a good relationship with him. If I was at the airport he would be the first one to come up and say hello. I think he just got stung a fair bit from the 2008 World Cup when the Kiwis scored [from his wild pass] and the papers came out with headlines like "Silly Billy", his relationship with the media changed a lot after that. From his point of view, all he did was keep the ball in play and he should have expected his Australian support to be there but they weren't. After that incident he was a little less open and giving.'

Journalist Brent Read laments the lack of access sports journalists have to players such as Billy in the modern game, which is highly controlled by marketing, media managers and player managers. 'Each club will wheel out six players a week and you might only get five minutes or so with them. Someone like Billy will only be available every three weeks or so and then only for a small time.'

Billy got himself into hot water in the press in 2010 for sledging. He was forced to apologise after an on-field incident with Newcastle player Cory Paterson, who was suffering from depression. In March of 2010, Billy allegedly said to Paterson during a game: 'Why don't you go to your room and have a cry?' Paterson's battle with depression had been publically highlighted for a while before the incident. Billy rang Paterson to apologise in person and then later apologised publically over the incident. Brent Read wrote in *The Australian*: 'Slater, who could also be heard chiding Paterson later in the match over his ability to give it but not take it, had already apologised to the Knights forward by phone on Sunday, but he reiterated his contrition yesterday in a statement released by his club.'

But such incidents and a number of suspensions have done little to tarnish the image of Billy, who has been able to keep one of the healthiest and homeliest profiles in league—a game whose image is brought down by rogue actions of out-of-control players almost every year. Billy has always been highly disciplined on and off the field.

* * *

Billy again starred in Origin 2011, scoring the winning try in game one when he ran off a Lockyer inside pass to score.

It was his tenth Origin try. It was part of a great comeback as New South Wales led the game with eight minutes to go. Billy was well on his way to erasing the previous year's bad memories.

In game two New South Wales bounced back to level the series with an 18–8 victory, but in game three Billy starred as the Queensland team bit back to run away with the game 34–24, Billy scoring off a Sam Thaiday pass in an historic match—Lockyer's last for Queensland.

In what became known as the 'Battle of Brookvale' on 26 August, Billy starred not for what he did playing but how he helped out an injured opposition player. The Storm were struggling and a huge all-in brawl erupted after a Storm player elbowed a Manly player in the face. Players converged and a wild melee broke out. In the aftermath Adam Blair for the Storm and Glenn Stewart for Manly were given ten minutes in the sin bin. But it didn't end there. As Blair and Stewart walked off they started arguing and then a fight broke out on the sideline. Even players sitting on the bench got involved as another melee broke out between the teams. Both Blair and Stewart were given their marching orders.

Meanwhile, in a chilling moment, Manly's 'Wolfman' Dave Williams went down in a tackle and Billy heard a breaking sound. Billy quickly cradled Williams' head in his hands, and tried to gain everyone's attention calling for a halt to play. Williams had fractured his neck.

'I knew straight away that there was an issue—because my right arm was on fire,' Williams said. 'That's when I couldn't move it and Billy held me. I didn't actually say anything when I hurt it. I was in pain and screaming and he said, "Don't move! Don't move!" He was telling everyone to piss off and trying to get the attention of the ref.'

Williams had fractured his c6 vertebrae and spent two months in a neck brace.

Billy was congratulated for his sportsmanship. Manly official David Perry said: 'The situation could be very different for the Wolfman if it wasn't for Billy,' Perry said. 'That's a medical fact. All of the players can learn from his actions.'

Manly coach Des Hasler rang Bellamy to pass on his thanks to Billy for his quick thinking.

* * *

The Storm ended the season on a high, finishing as minor premiers. They defeated Newcastle in the qualifying final but in a major upset, the Warriors lived up to their name by staging a surprise raid on the Storm at home ground AAMI Park to knock Melbourne out of the finals. Despite the loss, the Storm had answered the call to rise up again.

Slowly but surely Billy was climbing up the ladder of the greatest try scorers in the game behind the legend Ken Irvine with 212 tries (as of 2014, Billy was close to second on the all-time list. Pundits reckoned he would have to play for another three years to break the long-standing record). But he did have one record almost in the bag—highest try scorer for a fullback.

He earned the highest honour in Australia by winning the Dally M Medal. He had a series of strong games from round

19 to 24, which shot him to the top of the points table. Cooper Cronk finished in third place in the Dally M Awards, putting on notice he wasn't far off winning the medal.

Billy starred in the Four Nations tournament in England and Wales, taking out the International Footballer of the Year award as the competition progressed. But his tournament came to a grinding halt when he broke his right collarbone in five places during Australia's 36–20 win over England at Wembley. The game had only just started when Billy ran at full pelt to try and push England's Ryan Hall over the sideline with a shoulder charge but came off second best. Hall miraculously withstood Billy's charge and scored while Billy fell to the ground. Billy left the ground nursing his right arm in obvious pain. He'd smashed his collarbone to such an extent one broken piece was sitting on top of the other. He had to have surgery and a metal plate and pins inserted in his shoulder. He'd have the plate in for almost the entire 2012 season. Darius Boyd filled in for Billy in the final at Leeds on 19 November. Australia beat England 30–8 and left England deflated again, just when they thought their international league reputation was back on the ascendancy.

* * *

Billy would again miss most of the pre-season training as he recovered from surgery. He'd again face a long haul back to his peak for 2012. In the meantime, he sealed his long-term future at the Storm re-signing for another four years on a $400,000-a-year deal. It would mean he would end his career at the Storm and be one of those rare footballers to finish as a one-club player.

Roy Masters was again singing Billy's praises early in 2012—nine years after he had done so in Billy's rookie year when Masters instantly spotted Billy's potential. Billy was breaking all types of try-scoring records in the first few games of the season. 'He is tough and durable, returning quickly from a shoulder operation that was supposed to rule him out of the early season matches. He has superb ball sense,' Masters said. 'But players of all eras, clubs and positions celebrate Slater's skill and bravery. The Melbourne fullback has stepped into that magic realm few athletes enter. Basically, he does whatever he wants out there.'

Billy stunned everyone with his magic return from injury. By the start of April, he'd already scored 9 tries. Melbourne were again leading the ladder and it looked like this was going to be their season.

Billy had an ordinary Origin season, which finished in a huge disappointment when he had to rule himself out of the decider after a serious injury to his left knee. In game one of Origin, at Etihad in Melbourne, he was hardly seen and dropped the ball twice from high balls near his line, one of the mistakes leading to a Blues try. Queensland still ran out winners 18–10.

'You don't see him drop two in one game, so that might be it for him for five years,' Broncos coach Andy Griffin observed.

Then in game two, which New South Wales won 16–12 at ANZ Stadium, he suffered a serious knee injury; an injury he would be forced to battle with for the rest of his career.

Billy tweeted: 'Hi All, scans showed I've done my PCL in my knee. Looking at missing 4–6 weeks. Disappointed but I'm positive about getting it right. Thanks.' (Billy loved tweeting. He mixed in all his family life and Storm life and love of horses on his twitter feed. In 2014 he had about 113,000 followers on twitter.)

The posterior cruciate ligament injury would plague him through the rest of the season. Sometimes after a big game in the dressing room, Billy would have ice packs strapped to his knee, shoulder and thigh.

Billy set his sights on staging a miracle recovery for Origin game three. He didn't want to end his amazing run of fourteen consecutive Maroon games. But time ran out and he was forced to rule himself out of the big decider at Suncorp Stadium on 4 July. Only Billy could have thought he'd master such a bad injury in time for the big game.

Billy said:

> This was without a doubt one of the toughest and most frustrating decisions I have ever had to make. It just didn't feel right when I ran and I knew it wasn't going to be right, so I decided to do the right thing for my teammates and my own personal welfare by making myself unavailable. We didn't leave any stone unturned and I'm comfortable that we did everything we possibly could to get it right, but we were always racing the clock and there just wasn't enough time before Origin three.

Billy's body had copped a battering over the years. He was finding it much harder to recover. When he was a teenager he'd be right to go again after two to three days. But now the soreness set in for longer after a hard match. It might take him five or six days to get back to his peak. But, on the other hand, he was learning to be more careful with his body.

In one of the great Origin deciders at Suncorp Stadium in Brisbane on 4 July, Queensland just lasted to win 21–20, and frustrate the Blues again by a single point. The Blues' Josh Morris scored an amazing leaping try and then Todd Carney converted from the sideline to tie up the game at 20–20. Finally New South Wales sniffed an Origin series victory, a chance to bring the Queensland juggernaut to a halt, but it wasn't to be. It was Billy's great mate Cooper Cronk who broke the Blues hearts and the deadlock with five minutes to go, kicking a long range field goal almost from half way, which sailed smoothly and for Queensland, majestically, right between the posts. He'd kicked it with all the venom and skill he'd learnt practising football as a kid on his way home from school in Brisbane—in between hot chips. Now he'd won an Origin series doing the same thing. Billy was busy helping with the Channel Nine commentary team. Channel Nine appeared to be grooming Billy for a future career as a commentator. After the full-time siren, Billy rushed down from the commentary box in his suit to join in the celebrations with his Maroon teammates as they were handed the Origin trophy for the seventh time in a row.

Billy missed five games before he returned in round 21 against the Dragons. Despite missing games, he would still be Melbourne's top try scorer for the year with 16 tries. The Storm had a shocking run of five losses while Billy was out of play. After his return they didn't lose a match for the rest of the year, including the grand final.

The grand final against the Bulldogs on 30 September was a game of spite and needle in front of 82,900 people at ANZ Stadium. Billy went in on a Bulldogs try scorer with his legs and then Bulldogs players retaliated—one took him in a headlock and then threw him to the ground. In the ensuing melee, Bulldogs English player James Graham took Billy in a vicelike grip and appeared to be trying to bite his ear in a close clench. Billy was visibly upset and when he was asked by the referee Tony Archer if Graham had bit his ear, he replied, 'Yeah, f...in' oath … He bit me on the ear'. He showed Archer blood on his left ear. Graham was put on report.

Billy replied to the incident by scoring the next try for the Storm and then making a try-saving tackle. The incident had only pushed him to greater heights. The Storm led 14–4 at half-time and that was how the game finished, with no points scored in the second half. The Storm's trio of Smith, Billy and Cronk had overseen the Bulldogs attacking assault to win.

When asked by Phil Gould how the Storm won the game, Billy replied: 'Premierships are won on defence. That's what we build our game on. Defence, mate. Defence!'

There was no time for chest-beating from the Storm. Only a handful of players were still in the squad who had played in the 2009 premiership. Not even Bellamy jumped at the chance to stick the boot in to authorities for what had been done to the Storm. They were prepared to live on what they had achieved for the year, and leave it at that. They had adopted Masters' mental attitude of sticking with the positives of who they were, rather than dwelling on what had been done to them—and it had paid off incredibly quickly.

Of course, Billy's family was on hand for the big premiership win but, for the first time, Ronnie wasn't at the Olympic Stadium to watch his son. He'd been battling a bit of illness and instead was watching the game with a few mates at his Garradunga home in front of the big plasma TV.

He'd seen Billy put in a fabulous year. Ronnie always watched the footy and footy replays or the horses (he owns a couple of racehorses). What really had him up and running was Billy's great form in 2012, when Billy broke the all-time fullback try-scoring record of 129 tries held by Rhys Wesser. He then watched as the Storm overcame a form slump before the finals and then raced into the grand final against Bulldogs. On a warm steamy night in his home in the Far North, Ronnie and five mates watched Billy clinch his first official league premiership.

'I spoke to him on the phone straight afterwards and he was over the moon,' Ronnie said. 'Billy had a beauty, eh. That try he scored, it sealed it for them, I reckon. We've got three [premierships for Billy] now,' Ronnie added with the larrikin edge you'd expect from a Slater.

There was more to flow out of the grand final. Billy went up to Graham after the match and shook hands. Billy said later about the incident: 'It was behind me as soon as the game was over,' he said. 'Things happen on the rugby league field. There is a lot of emotion and I am a player who has done stuff and regretted stuff in the past, so I hold no grudges.'

Graham pleaded not guilty when he faced the judiciary the next week. He tried to absolve himself in front of the judiciary despite videos of the incident clearly appearing to show him trying to bite Billy's ear. 'I've played over 250 games, I've played since I was seven years old,' Graham said. 'I've never bitten anybody. I can't understand how anyone would think that I'd do that in an NRL grand final. I consider myself an honest person. I say honestly, I did not bite him.'

Graham said he was merely reacting to a fight situation and was clinching Billy so he wouldn't cop any punches:

> I'm not much of a striker ... I'm more thinking about being on the receiving end, getting as close as I can to stop them getting a punch on me. At that point in time, I'm just clinging. If I broke away from that, I've got a four-on-one situation. I'm just trying to stay in as close as I can.
> I just remember receiving a punch and trying to throw a punch, then I just remember players being on top of me and pulling me off.

The Bulldogs maintained the ear injury on Billy was probably from a scratch, not a bite. Just like the famous 'Bumper' Farrell incident during the 1940s, when Farrell was accused of biting a player and he protested he had no teeth, Graham showed his jumbled set of teeth to the judiciary also showing it wasn't a full set—so how could he bite?

But the judiciary only took ten minutes to find Graham guilty (unlike the rugby league committee back in the 1940s who found Bumper not guilty) and banned him for twelve matches. It meant he wouldn't play for the Bulldogs again until May, 2013. Graham flew home to Britain for Christmas ruing his Australian season.

The ear-biting incident produced some humorous headlines in the press, such as 'Bad Doggy', '"I'm a lover, not a biter", says Graham', 'Dogs bite worse than its bark' and 'Once bitten, the Storm has Dogs for breakfast'. Fairfax writer and Storm supporter Richard Hinds wrote '"Billy was once bitten, but not shy"—Billy scored a try soon after the biting incident'.

Billy had yet another international date after a grand final. For a change it was in his old home patch in North Queensland. Australia took on New Zealand in Townsville. The Kiwis again scared the hell out of Australia and in the rugged encounter three Aussies were injured including Inglis. Billy survived the helter-skelter game and Australia ran out winners 18–10, although the game could have gone either way.

Billy was looking forward to some rest and respite. Soon after all the victory celebrations Billy went to Spain to film an ad for his sponsor Adidas. Fortune again brought Billy back to the place where his athletic great-grandfather Juan Astorquia had come from.

'My nanna is actually full Spanish so I have a quarter Spanish in me. We told her we were coming over here, she is in Innisfail still and she was really excited,' Billy said.

He flew to Barcelona with Collingwood's Dale Thomas for the Adidas promotion for their new boot, the adizero.

Billy also went on holiday with his family to South Africa where he and Nicole shared a thrilling experience swimming in a cage dangled off a boat with great white sharks circling around them.

After the shark adventure and an African wild game safari, Nicole and Billy were soon back in the Far North to help prepare for Billy's sister Sheena's wedding in Cairns. Billy was also keen to do some spearfishing during his time off.

After one expedition the previous year he'd lumped a large lobster on to the kitchen table at Garradunga and said 'there you go dad'. Ronnie had looked back at him in shock. 'Where am I going to find a pot big enough to cook that thing in?' he exclaimed.

Unfortunately, the seas were too rough for Billy to indulge in his favourite sport over the summer break. With no spearfishing, Ronnie noticed the disquiet in Billy and by the second week of January he'd been called back to Melbourne to start pre-season training for the Storm. 'It's a good thing' said Ronnie, 'He was getting a bit fat eh,' he said with a laugh. The day after Billy left, the weather cleared and Billy's sister started her honeymoon, snorkelling on the islands off Cairns. 'Just the day after he left, it all cleared, he was real dirty when I told him, eh,' Ronnie said.

Returning to Innisfail was a big circuit breaker for Billy and his family. His extended family were there, his uncles, his cousins, and all the boys he'd grown up with at Goondi Bend.

He'd meet up with an old mate and go out for a punt up at the Brothers Club. He always loved the Innisfail annuals and one year he hired a private jet so he could get back there in time for the races. When he got around Innisfail, it was just like he was back in the fold.

He'd also been back home for the hard times after Innisfail was hit by cyclones, helping muster community support for the relief effort.

CHAPTER THIRTEEN

TOUGH AS TEAK

The new year gave Billy a chance to exorcise any old ghosts still haunting his career. Gradually he was taking back honours that had been taken away from him or had slipped out of his hands.

He quickly had another one in the bag. The Storm started the year on the best possible note—as the best club team in the world, after defeating Leeds Rhinos in February. A trim looking Billy (his birthday chum Smith was sporting a fair bit of holiday growth on his face, though) started the game at a cold Headingley field in England—a real shock for Billy after a Far North summer. And he started with a bang—breaking the Leeds line after just six minutes and almost scoring. He took two high ball screamers and looked safe as houses at the back. He then saved a try as Leeds tried to take the lead. In the twenty-first minute, the old Storm firm got into operation, Cronk sent Hoffman through the Leeds line and Billy was on hand to take the pass and score the first try. It was Billy's first full match of the year after a disrupted pre-season.

'I was a bit worried,' said Bellamy. 'He only played twenty minutes against Canberra [in a trial game] and he was really fatigued after those twenty minutes. He had a really good involvement. Some of the bombs he caught tonight were outstanding.' The Storm won the game 18–14 to take the world title.

Back in Australia, Billy found he was carrying some hurt from his Origin knee injury. This time it wouldn't go away as easily. He started the season well, though, scoring 3 tries against Brisbane. He kept his body trim and still played twenty-four games for the year—even more than Cameron Smith.

He hurt his foot in a game against Wests and wore a moon boot for the week leading up to the game against South Sydney. Everybody was talking about the match-up against his old Storm teammate Inglis.

Inglis had nothing but compliments for Billy. 'We all know and respect what Billy Slater can do,' Inglis said. 'As a football fan, I'd pay just to watch Billy Slater play. I've played with him and against him, and I can tell you it's much easier playing with him.'

Slater showed there was little wrong with his foot when he helped the Storm defeat Souths 17–10. But Souths would get their revenge in the finals later in the year.

Billy had a quiet Origin but again was part of a winning Queensland side—two close matches showed New South Wales was creeping closer to an Origin series win.

The Storm finished third on the ladder and Smith was pleased with how Billy was progressing going into the finals. 'I think the last few weeks we've seen the best of Bill and that's probably the best we've seen of him over the last eighteen months, ever since he injured his knee,' Smith said. 'He looks like he's running more freely.'

The Storm faced South Sydney in the qualifying final and everyone was looking towards the match-up between Billy and Inglis again. Billy had the edge on Inglis in several measurements during the season. Billy was coming off scoring 9 tries and 5 try-assists in his previous seven games before the qualifying final.

Before the finals, Billy had scored 17 tries to Inglis's 14 and had averaged 13.9 runs per game to Inglis's 11.8 for the year. But Inglis had made an average of 152.3 run metres per game compared to Billy's 135.5. (Billy would again be the leading try scorer for Melbourne in the season with 18 tries.)

But a 2012 repeat premiership was not to be. Souths won the qualifying final 20–10 and then Newcastle knocked the Storm out in the semifinal with a two-point win down at AAMI Park. It was the second time AAMI Park had proved a hoodoo finals venue for the Storm.

Billy had to cool his heels for a while. There was one big thing on his mind—the World Cup. It had been five years since the last one, when Australia lost in the final and Billy had made *that* throwback pass that gifted New Zealand a try.

He also had to gear himself up for a long time away from home, almost two months. It would be a tour of pain, agony and glory. Billy, of course, had to endure the usual media debate over whether Hayne should replace him at fullback and the continual questions about whether he wanted to overcome the bad pass in the 2008 World Cup final. But Billy brushed off all talk about overcoming ghosts or making up for the 2008 disappointment.

Before the team jetted off, Billy said:

> There's only a handful of us that were involved in that game and it was disappointing. World Cups don't come around too often and to let one slip was hard but we haven't talked about five years ago while we've been in camp. For the players that are here who were involved, then I'm sure that it's at the back of their minds. But it's not a motivation or a driving force for me. This is a World Cup and an opportunity to win, but I certainly won't be dwelling on the past.

The Kangaroos flew out to London on 14 October, and headed straight to their handsome digs in Manchester for a ten-day camp. Their first game was scheduled on 26 October in a World Cup opener against England in Cardiff. The Kangaroos had a lot of spare time on their hands and many observers saw the players were looking bored.

Their hotel wasn't a bad place to lob—a four-star hotel in the middle of Manchester, the Marriott Victoria and Albert Hotel, with luxury rooms, right near the ITV studios. The bar at the Marriott had many TV celebrities and public figures moving through. The Kangaroos would be there for almost six weeks and they were made to feel like part of the hotel family down by the river. A top Czech soccer team, Viktoria Pizen, was also staying at the hotel waiting for their Champion Leagues match against Man City.

But some close to the team observed that many of the squad seemed both 'bored and homesick'. It didn't seem clear why they were there so early, almost two weeks before the first game after already being in camp in Australia. 'It was a real problem to keep them focussed and you might have said it could have created an environment for some off-field incidents,' an observer said.

Australia's first game was up against one of the competition favourites, hosts England, at Millennium Stadium in Cardiff. More than 45,000 people turned out for the game in which Australia had to struggle all the way to defeat a determined England. Billy scored just before half-time as Australia put in 4 tries in an eighteen-minute spell. He dummied twice to beat the English defenders. Billy may have thought the World Cup ghosts were coming back to haunt him when Englishman Josh Charnley snapped up a loose pass from Billy and ran untouched to score. Australia managed to hold on 28–20. Billy was one of the best on-field, making 158 metres for the game, but strangely only making two tackles.

Billy was rested for Australia's next pool game against Fiji, which Australia won comfortably.

Their next match was against Ireland over the Irish Sea to be played on 9 November at Thomond Park in Limerick. And it would be the start of a painful week for Billy. The merriment of the Irish tour would eventually lead to a major public relations disaster back in Manchester and a late-night visit to a Manchester police station.

Australia trounced Ireland 50–0 before a pathetic crowd of 5000 as the Irish Wolfhounds were given a walloping. In one try, Billy ran through three Irish players to score untouched (his twentieth international try). Remarkably, he didn't make one tackle for the entire game, so flimsy was the Irish attack. The Kangaroos got to visit the Guinness brewery during their Irish sojourn and were in a merry mood when they were heading back to their Manchester base on a charter flight, having booked their place in the World Cup quarter-finals. Some of the Irish team came back with them on the plane. The Kangaroos were given a free hand to do what they liked on the Sunday. Coach Tim Sheens left it up to the players to use their own discretion on going out and didn't impose a curfew. Some of the Australians later kicked on to the Mojo bar nightclub in Bridge Street in inner Manchester, about five blocks away from their hotel. No-one thought it would end up in a donnybrook.

It was about 2am in the morning when Billy found he'd left his coat in the Mojo bar and went back to retrieve it. When he got there, there was a long line-up to go in and Billy started talking to the doorman. CCTV footage shows a man, later found to be a forty-year-old Manchester man, hitting Billy with an open hand. Billy then pushes him away with his right arm. Both men were detained and taken to the Manchester City police station. Billy was kept at the station for nearly five hours while CCTV footage was retrieved over the incident. Manchester police determined Billy had been provoked and acted in self-defence.

Manchester police said in a statement: 'One of the men threw a punch at the other, so the victim retaliated and punched him back in self defence.'

Australian team management released a statement saying: 'After reviewing CCTV footage of a scuffle outside a Manchester nightclub, police have determined Slater was the victim who acted in self-defence and have informed him of his right to press charges.'

Billy phoned up Nicole in Australia straight away to assure her he was okay. The alleged assault came as a huge public uproar grew in Australia over a spate of king hits outside Sydney nightclubs. Nicole rushed to his support with an Instagram message:

> Some man thought it was ok to punch my husband in the face, because he thought he pushed in line. If he had king hit him I would have to raise my 2 kids alone. What has this world come to? makes me sick, think before u act, there is a family behind everyone. And your actions in that 2 sec can change people's lives 4 ever. This has to stop.

In league forums debate raged whether Billy was actually a victim of a king hit. (Neither he, the police or the team camp had ever said this. The only reference to a king hit was from a *Daily Telegraph* report on the incident when it first occurred.) It looked more like an open hand push to the face. But it certainly showed Billy was provoked.

(The league integrity unit later investigated the incident and could come up with no new evidence.)

Billy fronted the media the next day and expressed his disappointment for taking the spotlight away from Australia's World Cup campaign. 'I think we have to be aware of the situations we find ourselves in,' he said. 'I suppose it is probably a bit of a wake-up call for everyone when we do go out.'

Billy didn't want to go into the details of the night and said he would not be pursuing police action against the man involved. 'I'm not going to sit here and go through the finer details of the events of last night. I think it has been well documented and the police report has the facts in it. I'm disappointed that [the] spotlight is on this and not the tournament and the games we've played. I just want to express my disappointment there and move forward.'

Sheens refused to comment on the incident at first—he seemed more upset the Australian players were out so late.

A few days later he told Australian Associated Press: 'Billy was returning to the venue to collect his jacket that he left behind when he was attacked. Both men were detained for several hours while police reviewed footage of the incident. He reacted the same way most people would. He was assaulted and he threw one back. He got hit first, doing nothing. What's that if that's not being a victim?'

Sheens said he had never contemplated standing Billy down over the incident.

It wasn't the only police incident involving the Kangaroos in Manchester. Josh Papalii was also robbed by a group of men after a late night out.

The Kangaroos regrouped for their quarter-final the next weekend at Wrexham against the United States. It was expected to be a walkover. But what should have been an easy training run turned into a major injury blow for Billy. During the 62–0 romp, Billy fielded a bomb and slightly held up his left knee as he was hit heavily by Tomahawks forward Roman Hifo. He immediately fell down in pain clutching his knee. It was the same knee he'd injured in Origin game two in 2012. He was helped off the field and could hardly walk. The swelling in his knee was massive.

'It seems like the same injury, I suppose that's a good thing because the PCL isn't functional anyways,' Slater said after the game. 'I suppose the only concern is the cartilage now and we'll know more from the scans.'

The prognosis was not good. He was immediately ruled out of the semifinals and it looked likely he would go home early.

Brad Walter saw the drama of Billy's injury unfold. 'Straight away as he got back from Wrexham the immediate diagnosis was that he was gone [from the tournament]. Sheens thought he was gone.'

Sheens started looking at his options to fly someone in to fill in for Billy for the last bit of the finals. Inglis would move to fullback and they needed a new centre. It was an awkward shake-up just before the big one (everyone assumed Australia would beat Fiji in the semifinal and go straight to the final). After Billy had scans they found the injury wasn't quite as bad as they had first thought. 'But he was only an outside chance to play,' Walter said.

Australia won against Fiji and were to meet New Zealand in the World Cup final. The Australians moved camp to London at the plush five-star Royal Gardens hotel, where the Wallabies and Australian cricketers often stayed.

The Kiwis were in hot form. But the Aussies were inspired—no-one on the team had won a World Cup.

'The Kiwis were looking pretty good and were very confident,' said Walter. Sonny Bill Williams was on fire and Walter described the Kiwis semifinal against England as the best match of rugby league he had ever seen. 'The Kiwis only got up to beat England in the dying minutes. It was just end to end stuff and then there was unbelievable defence. Sam Burgess was everywhere and that is the best performance by an England second-rower ever. Sonny Bill was unbelievable as well.'

Burgess made the most metres for any player on the field—173 metres—more than any back, an incredible performance. He was named man of the match and almost won the game for England with a try with fifteen minutes to go but the Kiwis came back with a try and conversion to take the match 20–18 in the last few minutes.

The Australians faced a ferocious Kiwi tide. The Kiwis even did a haka at an official World Cup function in Manchester before the final to try and send shivers down the Aussie team.

Meanwhile, behind the scenes Billy was battling around the clock to get back in time for the final. No-one gave him a chance. He only had fourteen days until the final to get fit— even less than that as he would have to pass a fitness test. He seemed like he didn't have a chance in hell.

Luckily, among the Kangaroo contingent was the Storm physio Tony Ayoub. He and team physio Steve Sartori worked with Billy night and day to get his left knee right. Ayoub had worked with Billy's injury problems since 2007. He knew how to put a footballer back together. Kangaroo Nate Myles offered a revolutionary US-designed ice compression machine called game ready for Billy to use. Billy used the compression treatment nearly every hour on the hour during the day until he fell asleep. The process would start again the next day from 8 am. Billy didn't leave his hotel room for almost a week. (The machine was attached to the injured leg. It was a cold compression device that increased blood flow, sped up healing and tissue growth, and reduced the time needed for pain killers.)

In the lead-up to the final, wealthy English businessman and rugby league club owner Marwan Koukash stepped into the breach when Australia needed a training ground. He offered up his Salford City's home ground as a training base. Koukash was the biggest racehorse owner in the United Kingdom and quite a character. He arrived in England as a refugee from the Middle East and built up a business from scratch based on company training. It skyrocketed in value and turned him into a billionaire. He bought struggling league club Salford Red Devils and was hoping to turn it into the next big thing in the English Super League. He put out feelers to get Billy and Kiwi superstar Sonny Bill Williams to join the club as marquee players. Koukash loved to watch Billy play and befriended him during the World Cup. They both, of course, shared a love of horses.

(Koukash named a horse after Billy. He simply called it Billy Slater. But the horse, in its early career, was nothing like the star footballer. It ran seventh and fourth at its first two starts and the form comment on its last run at Chester read: 'slowly away, outpaced, made some late progress'—almost the complete opposite of the human version. Koukash had some more honest horseflesh in his stable, including his galloper Mount Athos, which had run third in the Melbourne Cup in early November.)

It was on Koukash's Salford ground that Billy emerged from his intense medical treatment in his hotel room to perform a fitness test. If the test failed he was out of the final, with three days to go. He was still unsure if he should play or not. Remarkably, he passed the test and Sheens had enough confidence to slot him in as fullback for the big game. The game was played at Old Trafford in Manchester on 30 November in front of 74,468 people—a remarkable crowd considering the host nation England had been knocked out. The World Cup was well on its way to becoming a success after the financial debacle of previous World Cups, especially in 2000. It was at last resurrecting its profile and interest on the rugby league calendar.

Before he ran on the field, Billy ran up and gave team physio Tony Ayoub a huge hug. Ayoub had never seen him so emotional in more than six years of watching him play football. Before the players ran on they were given an unlikely extra incentive. The match day program was circulated for the final and inside the major league journalists and commentators were asked to nominate the best players in their different positions from the World Cup series. The only Australian nominated was Paul Gallen—chosen by Steve Mascord. Not even Billy was nominated as best fullback. The program was handed around amongst the Kangaroos before the match in the dressing room and it became a big talking point. They were livid. How could the names of the best side be left out of the list of best players? They were ready to prove themselves. Billy had never been so nervous going into such a big game. He knew he wasn't quite fit.

There was a massive roar as the Kangaroos filed on to the field. Instinct led to the first try. Billy, his left knee still tender, showed little sign of injury when he raced through the Kiwi defence and flew high to catch a ball off a Thurston bomb to score the first points. He couldn't have imagined a better outcome, a better start. The Kiwis quickly looked shattered and forlorn; the Kangaroos looked fresh and dangerous. Billy was backing up and running as he normally did and he was living out his long-held World Cup dream. Cooper Cronk scored a try after a mix-up amongst the Kiwi players and Australia led 16–2 at half-time.

Australia hit the ground running in the second half and so did Billy. He scored his second try after an Australian burst up the left side. He was there in support, his knee still hurting, pushing away Kiwi defenders trying to slow him down, and then taking the pass to fly over to score. If he had exorcised his ghosts he had done it then, as Australia had a massive lead. Brett Morris then scored two cracker tries, one after a Jarrod Hayne line break. In the first try, momentum took Morris into an advertising hoarding but he recovered to play on and then score another blinder. Billy made a number of mistakes at the end. He made two knock-ons both just 10 metres out from the Australian line, but New Zealand couldn't capitalise on the mistakes. Australia were too good and too quick and won the World Cup 34–2. It was, as one commentator said, a rugby league master class from Australia.

It was Australia's first World Cup title in thirteen years. Thurston was named man of the match.

Smith said he could not recall playing in a better Kangaroos victory. 'I may have told a little white lie in the build-up when I said this didn't mean too much from 2008. But standing out on the field after the match I think a little bit of the disappointment from 2008 was erased.'

Sheens said the senior members of the team had stood up. His gamble to play Billy had paid off. (It was a gamble, because if Billy fell heavily on his left knee during the game he was probably straight off the field and the Australian game would have been upset.)

Billy made 145 metres for the match, the third highest of any player, and had made seven tackles and four runs from dummy half. It was a superlative performance.

Billy told the press: 'I couldn't walk a week ago ... to get out there and perform the way we did was very special.' After the presentation Billy tried to give his World Cup medal to Ayoub in appreciation for what he had done. Ayoub refused to take it. Billy even slipped it into Ayoub's bag later, but Ayoub gave it back—again.

The Australians celebrated later at the Royal Gardens bar into the early hours of the morning. Some of the players were giving it to the press mingling in the bar, commenting on how they'd only put one of the Aussie players in the list for best team of the Cup, rubbing it in that they had taken the World Cup trophy. Greg Bird and Gallen were particularly vocal. They wouldn't let up. Ironically, it might have been just the motivation the Australians needed to win the Cup.

Billy was over the moon. He'd fulfilled a long-held desire and had capped his amazing career.

CHAPTER FOURTEEN

RIDING ON HORSES

It takes four people to get a life-size horse sculpture up the stairs of Nicole Rose's art studio in Richmond. Once it's standing in the studio the delivery people dust off their hands and look pleased with the job—all in one piece. Nicole will paint it for a shopping centre's exhibition of animal art. Nicole looks at it and considers the project ahead. She might paint it purple—an obvious choice—but she's done that before, on an elephant. She's in an African mood. Think bold and bright. She thinks perhaps she'll paint a zebra horse, bluish with red stripes, with slivers of yellow paint. Whichever way she goes it will be colourful.

Her little man Jake is running around the photographic art studio like it's a big playground. It's full of toys and play things—part of the studio props Nicole uses in her photography. She recently had a photo night for celebrities and Molly Meldrum was there too. She'd arranged for them to be photographed with some exotic creatures including a python. She likes bringing a bit of the exotic to inner-Melbourne.

Nicole has all kinds of commissions coming in. Out of the blue she's received a commission for some artworks for an art gallery in New York and she's busy at work on that project while keeping an eye on Jake. She thinks she'll paint some Australian wildlife, probably birds.

Nicole is thinking of family life after the hectic world of football. She hopes to run a farm with horses and provide horse lessons for kids and carry on her art. It could be in Victoria or further up the coast, it might even be in far away Queensland, back near home. Billy's already talked about being a small-time horse trainer and breeder. It's a lingering passion they share. The couple often visit horse studs and Billy had his picture taken with the retired Melbourne Cup hero Makybe Diva. He loves the thrill of racing and still has many friends in the industry.

It was no surprise the Slater family were chosen to be ambassadors for Victoria's summer-autumn racing. It promoted 'Relaxed Racing', but the horse they gave Billy to ride at the launch had other ideas. Maldivian was always a handful. The Cox Plate winner caused a sensation in 2007 when, as the red-hot favourite for the Caulfield Cup, he became fractious and reared up and hit his head on a TV microphone fixed by screws to the top of the barrier and carved a chunk out of his neck and head area. He was scratched from the race. But you'd think the horse, whose job now is to be a friend to little yearlings on trainer Mark Kavanagh's Gisborne farm, would be a little bit more relaxed in retirement. Nicole reckons Maldivian thought he was back to race when he was walked out on to the course proper at Caulfield. Billy dressed in jockey silks, with B Slater printed on his jockey pants, suddenly had to retrieve all his riding knowledge as Maldivian rose high and tried to buck him over the outside fence. Nicole never doubted Billy would bring the big gelding back under control. Billy was using all his might to cling on with just his toes in the stirrups. Nicole thought, 'mmm, this will get some publicity'. And it did. At least Tyla and Jake were given some quieter small ponies to ride at the launch.

* * *

Just a few kilometres from the studio, Billy is feverishly training at Gosch's Paddock outside AAMI Park with the Storm. He's running around the field with his baseball cap on backwards, his dodgy left knee strapped up, calling the shots, leading the way, jumping the ropes on the sideline. Bellamy has his arms folded, but isn't looking too hard or even yelling. It's like everyone knows what to do, so why should Bellamy holler anymore? There's a bit of hijinks. The Kiwi international Kevin Proctor sits on the head of Cooper Cronk when he's on the ground. Billy's the most vocal. He's like an assistant trainer. The players are fit and ready for another season where the Storm will be dangerous again.

Billy's career is as busy as ever. Among many things, he's promoting Australian bananas and has just helped launch a series of Billy Slater books for children. Many still call him Billy the Kid. He'll always have that child-like love of life in his step. Life is still full of adventure, and every time he scores he has that beaming smile, just as he did when he was a kid, scoring tries down at Goondi Bend. He's never lost the excitement and thrill of playing footy.

He's putting in his twelfth year for the Storm and he's still the Australian and Queensland fullback. His body has withstood a decade of bashing, but he's as eager as ever and doesn't look like stopping at thirty. It would take at least another three years for him to become the highest try-scorer in rugby league history, to beat Ken Irvine's 212 try record (a record no-one thought could ever be broken).

Irvine and Billy share a lot in common—speed, agility and humility. Irvine played for Norths and Manly, playing first-grade from 1958 to 1973. When he first appeared on the scene people said the same thing about him as they did about Billy. 'No-one knew what effect this lightly built kid would have on rugby league,' one commentator said. Irvine played on the wing but he was a ball player and great reader of the game like Billy. 'He had the knack of turning the half-chance into a try,' the commentator said. His love of playing for Australia mirrored Billy's. Once when Irvine ran away to score a try and help win the Ashes for Australia in England, the British caller said 'not even a high-speed handicap horse could catch this fella'. He also mirrored Billy's nature—totally self-effacing. If he did something fantastic on the ground, he'd say 'we did it'. The team came first.

It would be fitting if Billy could equal Irvine's record. No doubt if Billy achieved the feat—the highest try-scorer in rugby league history—he'd say he couldn't have done it without Cooper Cronk and Cam Smith and the rest of the Storm players over the years. Although it is such a long-held record sometimes an exceptional player like Slater comes along who rewrites history. It would be a brave person willing to punt against Billy not taking out yet another milestone, and reaching another great mark.